Monologues for Teens

60 Original Monologues to Stand Out, Inspire, and Shine

Monologues for Teens

60 Original Monologues to
Stand Out, Inspire, and Shine

Mike Kimmel

Foreword by Jean Carol

ISBN: 0998151319
ISBN 13: 9780998151311

Library of Congress Control Number: 2017918828

Ben Rose Creative Arts
New York - Los Angeles

Photography by Avis Wrentmore
Printed in the United States of America

First edition

Praise for
Monologues for Teens

"I am so impressed with Mike Kimmel's *Monologues for Teens.* I see the same scenes done over-and-over again, year-after-year. The scenes in Mike's book are perfectly geared towards today's youth. Actors constantly ask me what scenes they should show to a director. They should show us something unique, which is what you will get with the scenes presented in *Monologues for Teens.* I highly, and unequivocally, recommend this book. Hats off to you, Mike, for a fantastic collection of scenes for young actors. Actors will definitely benefit from this great resource."
– Tom Logan
DGA/SAG/AFTRA/AEA
Feature Film/Television/Commercial Director
Escape From Cuba, Bloodhounds Inc., Horse Play,
The Voucher, What If, The Neon Tiki Tribe, Dream Trap,
The Million Dollar Minute, Campin' Buddies, Karma,
General Hospital, Days of Our Lives, Capitol
Author, *How To Act And Eat At The Same Time*
Acting In The Million Dollar Minute

"Mike Kimmel is back with another excellent book for young actors. His latest book is *Monologues for Teens*. This book is truly unique and the young actors who use it are going to get much more than just a collection of monologues. Mike's monologues are entertaining and inspiring at the same time. The monologues harken back to a more innocent time, and while we can't go back, we can step forward and carry ourselves with respect, dignity and compassion for each other in the way Mike conveys with his writing and monologues. Mike shares his roots, his family and friends from New York City in the book in a way that is just such a pleasure to read. These young actors have been given a gift with this book. When Mike asked me to write a blurb, I didn't realize that I was also given a gift by reading these monologues. I'm far from my teens but there are a few of the monologues I will be rereading to inspire me in life."
– John Duffy
Film Producer, Director, Keynote Speaker
The Flag, A Sunday Horse, Beneath the Darkness,
Blood and Bone, Who's Your Caddy, The Thirst,
Veteran's Day, Western Conviction, Wonder Girls,
Bring Me the Head of Lance Henriksen
Professor, MBA Program in Film,
John Paul the Great Catholic University

"Having worked with Mike Kimmel, I know firsthand his dedication to his craft. He's both a joy and a pro on set. What strikes me most about his collection of monologues for teens is how "open" they are. Though they're full of detail, most allow the actor to fill in their own backstory and intentions. As an actor, the monologues sparked my imagination and provided plenty of opportunities for emotional content and even humor."
  – Laura Cayouette
  Actor, *Django Unchained, House of Cards, True Detective, Camera Store, Hate Crime, One Month Out, Maggie, Convergence, Dark Places, Kill Bill: Vol. 2, Green Lantern, Enemy of the State, Treme, Queen Sugar, Cold Moon*
  Author, *Know Small Parts, Lemonade Farm, The Charlotte Reade Mystery Series:*
  –The Secret of the Other Mother, –The Hidden Huntsman, –The Missing Ingredient

"Mike Kimmel is right on the money! These monologues are age appropriate, clean and reflect all that can be right with the world. There is depth and there is humor. I promise a young actor will be able to find the perfect monologues to suit them and the audition they might be going for no matter where they live on the planet. Now I want him to write them for older actors!"
  – Susannah Devereux
  Actor, *Iron Thunder, Jimmy Zip, Chasing Ghosts, Chronology, Fogg, Silver Twins, Those People, Opposite of Earnest,*
  Portrayed Diane Neilson in *Shortland Street,*
  South Pacific Pictures for Television New Zealand

"I think of Mike Kimmel as a genial subversive when it comes to finding ways to overturn conventional practices of training an actor. He is also an integral part of that community who observe children as they demonstrate their newfound knowledge. In his last two scene study books, the focus was on youngsters; now Mike has taken on the high school crowd with a text that is loaded with energy and precision, clarity and ingenuity. My students took on Mike's loving emblem with gusto and delight. Their partnerships with each other crackled through the material, which has a simplicity and a directness that is wildly sympathetic to youth-in-the-making!"
  – Dr. Henry Hoffman
  Artist-Teacher-Writer-Director
  New Orleans Center for Creative Arts
  USA Today's All-USA Teacher Team
  Director, Young Shakespeare Company

"Mike Kimmel's monologues serve a dual purpose. They not only provide great material for young actors to use for auditions, they are inspiring and motivational in nature, taking the actor and the audience on a journey of self-discovery! They are clean and appropriate for all audiences and the humor is delightful. As an inspirational speaker, I find they remind me of the types of stories that are used to support major points of the best keynote speeches. I highly recommend this book!"
  – Tina Guillot
  Toastmasters International District Director 2016-2017
  John Maxwell Certified Coach, Trainer, and Speaker
  Contributing Author,
  101 Great Ways to Compete in Today's Job Market

"This compilation of monologues is unlike any I've ever seen. Each is artfully crafted in such a way that there is enough drama and conflict for the actor to really delve deep and explore complex emotions and stories while still maintaining an undercurrent throughout the book of kindness, self-awareness, and positivity. Actors spend so much of their time involved in the rehearsal process getting to know what drives their character's thoughts and behaviors, and the characters in this book have much to teach the young actors playing them. I applaud Kimmel for creating a book where the material lends itself to an awakening and education for both the young actor during rehearsals and also for the audience during an audition or performance."
– Misty Marshall
Sony recording artist
SAG/AFTRA, LA Music Commission Board
Executive Director, Empowerment thru Arts, LLC

"I've enjoyed reading and re-reading these pieces! They're each memorable and smart. I especially loved 'Something Happened,' 'My Deep, Dark Secret,' and 'Can I Be Honest With You?' The speakers are keen observers and thinkers, and every teenager I know craves recognition as a keen observer and thinker. Mike nailed his target demographic; I expect teens will enjoy embodying these characters. The dark subject matter also works. The thorny stories always finish with a motivational twist (become the hero of your own story; look at your problems one at a time; have patience with people you meet). Great idea! Thanks to the inspirational spin, the dark stuff never feels hopeless or gloomy."
– Eva C. Nusbaum
President
New Orleans Toastmasters

"Mike Kimmel has a calling to help people who want to act. He's helping actors from all walks of life, especially young, beginner actors. He's been around the block. He knows his way around the film or TV set. We met more than 15 years ago doing a skit on *The Tonight Show with Jay Leno*. I knew immediately this guy is a positive force. Hope you enjoy his latest book!"

– Ben McCain
TV Host, Actor, and Producer
My Name is Bruce, House of Cards, Homecoming,
Bio-Dome, Martial Law, Black Scorpion, Nashville Now,
Lois and Clark: The New Adventures of Superman, Julian,
The Pretender, Dead End, Hee Haw, Killer Tumbleweeds

"Where can teens find that perfect monologue for acting class or auditions? Well, look no further! HERE. IT. IS. The inimitable Mike Kimmel – aka *Mighty Mike* – is the consummate actor, teacher, writer – and the best acting mentor anyone could find. Mike is inspiring and intuitive, and the scenes and monologues he has crafted offer teen actors the materials they need to advance their skills and build successful careers – whether focused on a professional acting career, competitions, or an educational path. *Monologues for Teens* is a must-have for agents, casting directors and teachers, too! Definitely add this one to your coaching tool chest."

– Sharon Garrison
Actor, Producer, Acting Coach
Claws, Preacher, Midnight Special, Bomb City, Too Much
Pitch Perfect 2, American Horror Story, Salem, #am/pm
Game of Silence, Common Law, Sordid Lives, 1 Interrogation
Portrayed Judge Amelia Sanders on AMC's *Drop Dead Diva*

"Mike Kimmel writes from the heart, and these monologues are lovely reflections on life. They are humorous, introspective, and full of quirky anecdotes and musings. The pizza guy in "It's All About The Pizza" is a role model of humility and service. "Creatures of the Night" are the rats and mice that haunt the subway tracks in the wee hours and block our progress on the train of life. "Personal Hygiene" is a straightforward plea to remember the roll-on! We live in a time of cynicism and snarkiness where it's hard to find material that is appropriate for teens. I'm happy to say that Mike Kimmel's book IS appropriate for teens. I guess the big difference that I see between these monologues and other material that's supposed to be meant for this age group is that these pieces are generally hopeful. There is a thread of optimism that seems to tie them together. That's not to say that there are neat, tidy answers to the many questions posed here. Not at all. There are loose threads everywhere. That's life, after all. But there's also a light at the end of the tunnel. There is hope. And that, more than anything is the message in this volume."

– Roxanne Hernandez-Coyne
Voiceover Actress and Audiobook Narrator
Time Warner Cable, Bell South, GTE, Seaworld,
The Queen Mary, Comerica Bank, Jafra Cosmetics,
Best Western, *Saints Row, Ender's Game Alive*

"Mike Kimmel's Monologue Book for Teens is a must have for every teenage actor. Finally, a book of monologues that has depth and meaning, something teenage performers can sink their teeth into and is age-appropriate. Mike's years of experience as a writer and actor shine through in this collection. I highly recommend this book for those who are serious about their craft! Thank you, Mike, for creating material that inspires and gives young people in our industry the tools to help them grow both as actors and as human beings."
– GiGi Erneta
Actor, Host, Writer, Producer
Flag of My Father, When the Bough Breaks, Risen, Dallas, Happy Death Day, Too Close to Home, Jane the Virgin, American Crime, Queen of the South, NCIS: New Orleans, Scandal, Friday Night Lights, Veronica Mars, Crossed

"It is no surprise that from the mind of Mike Kimmel comes another wonderful book of inspiration, motivation and education. This time around, Mike has shared a fun, entertaining and exciting ride through his *Monologues for Teens.* It is refreshing to hear an author write so deeply from his heart (and mind) with such sensitivity and passion for what the reader will experience. Once again, Mike's work is thought provoking and we can deeply appreciate that we will walk away enlightened and thrilled by these stories. Most importantly, the "Teens" will enjoy and treasure this gift for many years to come."
– David J. Breland
Technology Specialist
Senior Project Manager
The Freeman Companies

"Mike Kimmel's *Monologues for Teens* is a very helpful resource for young actors. Finding a monologue to perform can be overwhelming. I've personally spent countless hours searching for something unique. *Monologues for Teens* has a wide variety of original monologues for actors to choose from for class or auditions. Teens, look no further, you're bound to find a great monologue in this book."
– Morgan Roberts
Actor/ Director, *Dynasty, NCIS: New Orleans, Ravenswood, The Inspectors, My Father Die, The True Don Quixote, When The Game Stands Tall, American Horror Story, Zoo*

"Mike Kimmel's *Monologues for Teens* are insightful and meaningful with a nice touch of humor. The teens can be a rough time, and Mike writes these monologues with an empathetic yet inspiring voice. I wish I'd had them available to me when I was a teen!"
– Kelly Lind
Actor, *The Big Short, Bad Moms, The Hollow, The Iceman, Preacher, NCIS: New Orleans, Different Eye, Treme, The Astronaut Wives Club, My Crazy Ex, Swamp Murders*

"It does my heart good to see someone in the acting profession who is giving something back. Mike is doing valuable work on behalf of newcomers with this book series. I've enjoyed reading through these monologues. They have very powerful messages written between the lines. I know they will benefit teenage actors tremendously."
– Johnny Valiant
Professional Wrestler, WWE Hall of Fame
Three-Time World Tag Team Champion
Portrayed himself in *The Wrestler* with Mickey Rourke

For Ben Ross and Aaron James,
who put the great in great-nephew.

"Do your little bit of good where you are;
it is those little bits of good put together
that overwhelm the world."

– Desmond Tutu

Table of Contents

Foreword

When longtime actor friend and writer Mike Kimmel asked me to pen a brief foreword for his new book, *Monologues for Teens*, I enthusiastically accepted. In the nearly two decades I've known Mike, I have come to know his terrific talent as an actor, a skilled and insightful writer and a passionate, inspired educator. Besides all of that, he's a downright, genuine nice guy. What an honor to be associated with his latest book.

The assignment caused me to reflect on a very basic question. Why do teens want to act? What on earth motivates them to dive in to such a demanding, competitive, soul searching, often frustrating performing art? Heaven knows there are thousands of other things to do in that interim known as puberty, especially in the age of technology.

Having been an actor since childhood myself, the answer seemed pretty clear to me. We act because we must. Because we are driven. Whatever personal differences we may have, we all share a deep urge, a strong, compelling need to explore our imaginations, discover and examine our inner selves, and our world and communicate the experience. Our thoughts, feelings, beliefs, emotions, are the paints for our canvas and the performance is our artwork. Acting is the action that brings the experience to life for us and our audience. It's not about "showing" – it's about sharing a truthful insight or experience.

When that irrepressible desire to take action and embark on the journey of discovery and self expression through acting erupts, what can aspiring actors do? What's the first step to channel their curiosity, expanding awareness and sensitivities into constructive action? Couldn't there be a road map or guide posts to help unlock the secrets of how to begin?

An actor's road can be a fascinating adventure and what Mike Kimmel has done in *Monologues for Teens* so beautifully is to lay out a series of sixty dramatic and comedic monologues expressly designed for teens to embark on their journey. The beauty of his writing is its simplicity and practicality. Its simplicity is found in its clarity and singleness of purpose. It's relevant, easy to read, speak and understand. It's relatable to the teen audience of today.

At the same time, his focus and message is refreshingly constructive and positive. How often did my master acting class teachers remind us that the true talent of an actor is never showcased in angry, ranting, one dimensional characterizations. Rather, good acting is the ability to express a range of human emotions that reflect many impulses, yearnings, fears, hopes and dreams, doubts, loves and hates, humor, silliness, curiosity, vulnerabilities and more. In other words, characterizations that reflect real people in a real world. Mike's monologues offer so many opportunities to develop multi-dimensional characters in a short scene.

Practically speaking, the monologues in *Monologues for Teens* are ideal for use as audition pieces, self-taped submissions, demo reels, for showcase situations, agent presentations and acting class exercises. Actors can self-tape these monologues and study and improve their own performance, too.

Remember, there is *never* only one "right way" to act a scene. Each actor must bring their own unique perspective to the role. So read this book. Work on these monologues, make them your own, enjoy the journey, be inspired by it, keep your work personal, truthful and real, and always strive for more.

Thank you, Mike Kimmel, for your amazing talent and insight in producing such a great gift for young actors everywhere.

Jean Carol
Los Angeles, California

Acknowledgments

A million thanks to Mollie, Adele, and Tammy, my three wonderful sisters, for always being so kind, gracious, and supportive.

Many thanks to Kimberley Bliquez, GiGi Erneta, Sharon Garrison, Tina Guillot, Orlee Hadari, Roxanne Hernandez, Misty Marshall, Eva Nusbaum, Joyce Storey, Erik Beelman, Stephen Bowling, David Breland, Francis Ford Coppola, John Duffy, Dr. Henry Hoffman, Tom Logan, Ben McCain, Morgan Roberts, and Johnny Valiant for encouragement, inspiration, feedback, and rock solid advice.

Very special thanks to Jean Carol for the thoughtful and heartfelt foreword to this book. Jean's talent, work ethic, integrity, and professionalism have inspired me often – and deeply – through the many bright years of our friendship.

Introduction

I believe actors have developed a love-hate relationship with monologues. We love performing monologues, knocking them out of the park, and leaving our audiences speechless. But actors can grow weary of the endless repetition of practicing monologues – and continually seeking out new material.

That's understandable. I've heard monologues called "a necessary evil." I never liked that description. If something is necessary for us, then it's intended for our good. It's intended for our well-being. I think monologues fit the bill, but definitely understand how the process of selecting, rehearsing, and performing monologues can feel tedious, arduous, and uncomfortable.

There's a simple but effective way around this. Don't think of your monologue as a speech or presentation you're delivering to an audience. Instead, think of it as a way in which you're finally permitted to talk out loud to yourself in public. You're not talking to an agent, casting director, teacher, or audience. You're talking to yourself. Think of a monologue as a private moment performed in public. This is helpful in getting us "out of our heads." It helps us become less self-conscious and more self-confident. You still want to apply your performance and presentation skills for the benefit of the audience, of course. This is how we demonstrate our command of movement, physicality, and vocal variety.

However, if you will begin to think of a monologue as your own personal inner dialogue – spoken out loud – you can alleviate much of the pressure actors put upon themselves in audition settings. Actors must learn to be comfortable in their own skin. Working on monologues is an excellent way to enhance and develop that sense of comfort and self-confidence. You will find that developing skill and confidence with monologues – like working on public speaking techniques – will benefit you in many other areas of your life, as well.

A monologue should have a clearly defined beginning, middle, and end. You will probably notice that the monologues in this collection are laid out in shorter than normal paragraphs. This is meant to provide added clarity and help you break each monologue down into manageable sections. The frequent paragraph breaks will assist you far more than if you were reading these pieces printed out in overly long passages.

Each paragraph break indicates a new thought, idea, reaction, or change in intention. This is commonly called "a beat," and denotes a pause or change in direction an actor takes with the script. Many playwrights will even write these pauses or shifts in action and intent into their scripts as stage directions in parentheses and italics (*beat*). The same effect, however, may be more easily accomplished by breaking a monologue down into shorter passages.

Adding an ellipsis (…) within the body of the dialogue assists in a similar manner. The ellipsis, or series of three periods, is a punctuation tool generally used in academic writing to indicate an omission in the text. In informal writing, however, we may also use the ellipsis to indicate pauses in action or changes in the speaker's thought process. Like frequent paragraph breaks, the ellipsis is relatively unobtrusive, allowing the actor to focus more fully on the script, character development, and backstory (rather than an unseen author or director's staging preferences).

Stage directions written into actors' dialogue, in fact, are frequently overused. They also tend to complicate scripts unnecessarily. Stage directions can make written dialogue become unwieldy and interfere with the actor's own creative process and original choices. These two very simple techniques – frequent paragraph breaks and using the ellipsis – will help you immediately in organizing and breaking down your monologue into more workable and easily digestible portions. They will help your monologue flow more naturally and without visual interruption through an author's written "beats" or description of specific actions to follow.

Additionally, it is an unfortunate fact that much of the material written for young people over the years has been negative, sarcastic, and even mean-spirited. This is truly regrettable, because I've always given teenagers much more credit than that. I've always believed teens can do better. All of us can do better.

Many scenes and monologues written for young actors over the last twenty years have been argumentative, demeaning, and even insulting. Many contain bad language and are overly pessimistic in style and tone. I believe this tendency comes from a desire to promote "edgy" material and shock the audience.

Edgy material definitely has its place in the entertainment industry. Audiences worldwide enjoy powerful, dark, and edgy scripts for stage and screen. For audition purposes, however, it's dangerous and unwise to go too far in this direction – particularly when the performer is a minor. And actors frequently go too far in this direction, believe me.

Try putting yourself in the shoes of a director, producer, talent agent, or casting director who must listen to audition monologues from strangers for a full day. Young actors can make these people uncomfortable by dragging them down into overly dark places emotionally. It's never a good idea to make the people who hire us uncomfortable. I've seen monologues for young people detailing actions that included bullying, academic cheating, theft, violence, and other unsavory intentions. Too much anger, angst, and aggression makes industry professionals uneasy. It makes them tune the actor out. It also leads them to see the actor as being overly self-indulgent.

The monologues in this collection are intended to convey a more uplifting message for your audience. They are meant to encourage positive behaviors and attitudes. When a heavily dramatic situation is considered, as in "Those They Left Behind" or "Something Happened," then a moral to the story is suggested, as well. This gives the actor an opportunity to deliver a thought-provoking message – rather than just wallow around on stage in a self-indulgent swirl of negativity.

I invite young actors to try something new and different beginning today. Try your best to be the actor who is an uplifter and an encourager in people's lives. I promise this will make you stand out in the crowd. Why? Simply because very few people ever make an effort in this area. People (of all ages) can become so focused on their own problems and difficulties, they fail to see one of the best solutions available to all of us. One of the most effective ways to fight through our own challenges in life is to help another person overcome his own. Robert Louis Stevenson advised us to "hide your fears, but share your courage." It's still great advice more than a hundred years later. This way of thinking (and acting) will make you memorable on stage, on screen, and in life. It will help make you a great collaborator too. Will this approach always work for you? No, unfortunately, but we miss one hundred percent of the shots we never take.

Voicing encouraging, thought-provoking messages through audition monologues enables you to create a positive impact – and become an active force for good – in the lives of people experiencing personal struggles and daily challenges. This is not the primary goal of your audition, of course, but it's a subtle and extremely effective secondary goal. Through the process of doing this, you put your best foot forward in the audition room. You present yourself to industry professionals as a stronger, more capable, more confident person than they normally meet. And what kind of director wouldn't want to cast that kind of teenage actor in his play, film, or television program?

I hope you will take this advice to heart. I hope you will apply it diligently in your auditions and your personal life too. I hope you will delve deeply into these monologues and use them to connect with your audiences in a powerful way. Most of all, I hope you will find blue skies, green lights, and the very best of everything on this exciting new road you are traveling.

Mike Kimmel
Los Angeles, California

A Note on Comedy and Drama

Some of the monologues in this book can not be easily categorized. They are not exclusively comedy or drama monologues. Some are dramatic with a comedic twist. Others are comedic, but with an underlying dramatic message or a touch of irony to give you – and your audience – something deeper to think about.

This is a lot like life. Experienced directors, producers, writers, agents, and casting directors understand this principle well. That's why you'll often see funny lines or comedic moments in an otherwise dramatic movie scene. The best example is in your favorite action film, which likely stars a reluctant hero with personal idiosyncrasies who wisecracks his way through overwhelming odds en route to saving the world. Similarly, your favorite comedy film probably has a terrific, very heartfelt moment with the star revealing something deeply personal about himself. This is a dramatic interlude that explains his lighthearted, comedic attitude and endears him to the audience.

Some of the monologues are clearly comedic and others definitely dramatic. But don't be overly concerned about placing them into one of these two categories if you don't see an obvious fit. All the monologues have a little bit of subtext – or an underlying theme or message – beneath the surface of the main idea. The most important thing is to deliver your monologue honestly and realistically, and explore the subtext – without overdoing it – to give your performance range, power, and depth.

We Might Have Even Been Friends

I saw this kid getting off the bus yesterday. Dressed like me. Looked like me. It was weird. This kid was getting off the bus when I was getting on. So we were kinda like ... right in each other's way. It was awkward for a minute.

So I just laughed. I said, "Sorry. My bad." And this kid didn't say anything. This kid who looked like me, dressed like me, wouldn't even answer me. Just looked me in the eyes ... real cold ... real hard, like I was a threat. Like I was an enemy or something. I don't know how to explain it.

Told you it was weird. Weird enough to make me think. I couldn't get it out of my head all day long ... this strange little interaction at the bus stop early in the morning.

I'm not a threat. I'm not anybody's enemy. Really, I'm not. I think I'm a pretty good person. I don't mean that in an arrogant way. I'm not the best student. I'm not the best athlete. I'm not anybody's role model, and I'm not trying to be.

But I am trying. Honestly, I am. Trying my best. I always try my best. I help at home. I watch my little sister after school. I return my library books on time. I always eat my vegetables. Well, almost always. Except when my mother makes cauliflower, but you can't blame me for that. She smells up the whole house with that cauliflower. I hate cauliflower.

What I'm trying to say is ... why do some people act so unfriendly? Why would people choose to live their lives like that? Like everyone they meet is an enemy. I don't understand.

Because I'm not that kid's enemy. If we met some other way, if we didn't have that strange little interaction on the bus ... we might have even been friends.

1

Employee of the Month

My grandfather says it's important to become an observer of human nature. I always think about that. I try to understand what he means. And when I do, I start to notice stuff.

Like yesterday, I was with my mom at the store. And this lady who worked there was ... how do I explain it? Not exactly rude to my mom. But not nice, either. Definitely not nice. My mom asked a question and this lady looked like she couldn't be bothered. She answered my mom ... but she kinda made a face. Kinda rolled her eyes too.

And my mom didn't say anything to me. My mom hardly ever complains ... but I know she wasn't happy about it. I could tell this lady really hurt her feelings.

Sure, the lady did her job, but she just wasn't too nice while doing it. Niceness counts. It counts a lot.

Then I remembered Grandpa's idea about being an observer. And I looked on the wall near the cash registers. They had this big sign – *Employee of the Month* – with pictures of the workers. One for every month. This lady's picture wasn't up there. Right. Surprise, surprise.

I thought ... these are the workers who try real hard. Who do their best. Who act nice to all the customers.

So after my mom paid, I showed her that sign. And I said, next time let's get the Employee of the Month to help us. I don't think the lady who helped us was trying too hard to get her picture up on that board.

So my mom kinda smiled. And then she took me for ice cream. If my mom worked at that store, she'd definitely be Employee of the Month. Personally, I think she's also Mother of the Year.

The Green Pencil

You know those little, tiny pencils? Golf pencils, I think they're called. The kind they have at the library. Those little itty bitty ones. Yeah. Those.

I was in the library researching a paper. Wasn't even using the Internet. Just going through the stacks. Old school style, through the print books. Writing down stuff. That's why I needed a pencil.

So I go to the desk. They have a little box of pencils. I look inside. What do I see staring back? Whole bunch of little yellow pencils ... and right on top is ... a green one. A tiny green pencil. All by itself. I never saw a little green pencil. What the heck is it doing there? I didn't know they make 'em in different colors. I've only seen yellow. One of a kind, for sure.

It made me think. We're like that little green pencil. We know we're supposed to stand out. Deep down, something tells us our nature is to be unique, one of a kind ... individualists. We don't always follow through. Do we?

Einstein said everyone's a genius. But if you judge a fish by its ability to climb a tree, that fish will spend its whole life believing it's stupid. I know this about you. You didn't show up to be another yellow pencil in the same old, same old box.

This world doesn't need more yellow pencils. We have enough. We need more green pencils writing their scripts and casting their marks on this funny little planet of ours. Become a green pencil.

Be the one green pencil in that box of yellows. Be an original. Start today. Get your fire back. Write yourself an exciting life adventure with that pencil you discover inside, that unique different color pencil you've always known deep in your heart that you truly are.

Puppy Dog Eyes

We got a new dog. Mom and Dad didn't like the idea. I can't blame 'em. We already have two. But what's one more? Not a lot more work, right?

He's a rescue. We went to the pound, and I couldn't resist. This little dog had the cutest little droopy smile.

It's kinda funny saying we got a new dog because he's really an old dog. Oldest dog at the shelter. Maybe the oldest dog on the planet.

He just creaks along, walking really slowly ... all hunched over. Kinda like my grandpa does.

But if you look closely ... when you look in this old dog's eyes ... that's when you really see something. When you see him smile ... when you see him smile that little droopy smile ... he looks just like a puppy.

Got the cutest little wiggly nose too, and those big, brown eyes. With a little twinkle, a little sparkle. Yeah, he looks just like a puppy when you look deep into those eyes. He doesn't look like a puppy when he walks – and creaks along – but you see the puppy when you take the time to look in his eyes.

Guess that's where we get the expression "puppy dog eyes."

But, like a lot of things in life, many of us miss it. We don't see it unless we take the time. And to see something special, something beautiful, really takes time. So I take the time. I take the time every day.

Because he's my new dog. My new old dog. My new old dog with the droopy smile and the puppy dog eyes.

He just walks a little slower than our other dogs ... but that's okay.

It's okay. Because he helps me slow down. I'm keeping up with him. Everything doesn't have to be such a rush. I'm taking my time now too.

Something Happened

I remember my Uncle Johnny – my dad's little brother – talking about the day Grandpa died. That was my dad's dad. And Uncle Johnny's dad.

Uncle Johnny was only twenty-two years old when it happened. He was in the house the day Grandpa had his heart attack. He called the ambulance.

And then – he told me – he drove really crazy following that ambulance too. He was driving and trying to hold back his tears at the same time. Driving and crying and praying. He pulled out of the driveway real fast … and drove down the wrong side of the street to catch up to that ambulance.

Uncle Johnny tells everybody that was the most stressful day of his whole life. He was running around like a maniac. He admits it. Says anybody who knows him wouldn't even recognize him if they saw him that day. He was … so crazed … so amped up … anyone who knew him wouldn't recognize him.

But what if you didn't know him? What if you were a stranger? What then?

What if the first time you met Uncle Johnny was on the day his father died? His father, who was also his best friend.

What would you think about my uncle if that's how you met him? What kind of first impression would he have made? Think about that next time you see someone acting … not quite right.

Before you judge them … before you get mad … just remember that person might be going through some stuff. Might be dealing with things you can't know about.

A lot of people are hanging by a thread. So have patience with everyone. Cut people a little slack, okay?

Maybe the day you meet someone … that someone's having the most horrible day of his life. Maybe that's the day something happened.

Social Skills

You know what the problem is? With people my age. My generation. You know what our problem is? No? I'll tell you.

We. Have. Lost. Our. Social. Skills.

Lost the ability to connect with people. We don't talk to each other any more. We chit-chat, but that's not the same. We don't connect like people did years ago.

We connect with our phones. We connect with our tablets. We connect with our devices.

Hey, I'm guilty of it too, believe me. But at least I'm aware. I try not to give in to temptation every time I hear that thing start beeping in my pocket. I don't have to answer every time. I am more than capable of resisting. Now, I can't say I'm perfect. But I'm trying, and I'm definitely getting better. Because it's a process. It's a skill, a muscle we can develop.

That's why I tell my friends to make an effort. Put away your phones and connect with people! Make eye contact. Say good morning. Say "please." Say "thank you." Hey, here's one for you. Say "you're welcome." When was the last time you heard "you're welcome" when someone said "thank you?" Probably never, because nobody says "thank you."

These are called "pleasantries." Simple verbalizations we can use every day just to make life a little nicer. Imagine that. Because we're all human beings.

And because it's important to be more aware of our surroundings. It's important to connect with one another on a personal level. We all need that personal connection. Over time, that helps develop our social skills.

Some of my friends even take their phones into the bathroom when they go. I mean ... seriously?! Come on, people! Disconnect! Focus! Don't you need both your hands free?

Social skills. That's right. We need to develop better social skills. Not social media skills.

We've got those down. Pretty sure we're good to go with those.

Taming the Monsters.
Silencing the Chatterboxes.

D o you ever have negative thoughts? I think a lot of people struggle in this area. More than you realize. Really negative. Like little enemies whispering to us.

Telling us stuff that's not good. Stuff we can't do, things we can't have. Telling us we're not good enough, smart enough, capable enough.

My mom calls it our little mental chatterbox. My dad calls those thoughts ... the monsters in his head. Best description I ever heard. I think we all have them too.

Negative little chatterboxes. Like little voices whispering to us, putting us down.

Those thoughts, those monsters must be tamed, my friends. They create stories for us, stories most of us believe – without ever questioning them, without ever challenging them.

I think the saddest thing in the world is that so many people listen to those stupid little chatterboxes. That's why people give up too soon, too early ... right before they reach the finish line. That's why people quit pursuing their goals and their dreams in life.

The good news is that like the monsters in every story, every fairy tale, every video game ... they lose. They lose and we win. The monsters always lose.

The best way to tame the monsters in your head is to become the hero of your own story, the knight in shining armor coming to your own rescue, the cavalry leading the charge to save the day.

I want to encourage you to transform yourself. Become the hero in your own story today. Be your own unbeatable warrior.

You are the world's greatest living expert on you!

Nobody knows better than you what you want, and what will make you happy. No one is more capable than you of taming the monster, slaying the dragon, silencing that ugly little mental chatterbox inside your own head.

The Shortest Guy in Class

School was weird today. Some kids were making fun of this new student. He just transferred from another school. Nice boy. Friendly kid. A little quiet.

And definitely very … short. Yeah, he's short enough that a lot of kids were putting him down. Don't worry, I didn't participate. I never do that. We shouldn't make fun of people because of their appearance. It's not like they can control it. This guy can't decide what height he can grow to, can he?

I told my mom when I got home. Mom had an interesting perspective. She said … if we watch this kid throughout the school term … we'll see a pattern emerge. She says never overlook the shortest boy in class. Girls too, by the way. Don't be so quick to write them off. Kids like that always work harder. Maybe they have something to prove and it makes them try a little harder. Maybe a lot harder.

They have a name for it. They call it *The Napoleon Complex*. Okay, Napoleon was not a nice guy. Did a lot of bad things. I get that. But he could have done a lot of good things. That's on him. But it doesn't matter. That's not the point. The point is he was motivated. And one of the things that motivated him was a desire to prove himself. To do great things and overcome his height.

Lots of famous people were short and still accomplished some pretty amazing things. This new kid might turn out the same way. So I'm just saying … don't be so quick to write him off. Don't overlook him because of his height.

Watch his progress throughout the semester. He won't be captain of the basketball team. But there may be another area in which he will become a giant … and more than measure up.

The Secret of Dogs

D o you like dogs? Me too. My whole family likes dogs. Sometimes, when I'm walking my dog, someone comes up and asks if it's a girl or a boy. I say – "*Neither. It's a dog.*"

Really, I don't even like calling a dog "It." I call a dog "He or She." Because "It" sounds like an object. And a dog is nothing like an object. Except a dog is the object of my affection. And my appreciation. Dogs are special and unique. In all the animal kingdom, no other species connects and bonds with us in that rare, beautiful way that dogs like to do.

Imagine an owl or a hippopotamus or a porcupine living in your house, waiting for you to feed them, and running up and wagging their tails when you walk through the door. Sounds kinda weird, right?

But think about it. Isn't it just as bizarre to see dogs – another completely different species – acting the way they do towards you and me?

What is it dogs like so much about us? About humans? My Uncle Charlie says he prefers the company of dogs to human beings. I'm not sure I'd go that far, but it probably depends on the human being. Uncle Charlie says he even prefers porcupines to some human beings.

I think dogs have a secret. They have a super power that no other animal has. Dogs can see the very best in us. Dogs don't see us as we are, but as we would like to be. Dogs think we're perfect. They appreciate us. They appreciate everything we do for them. That's why they try so hard to please us … and to be man's best friend.

I think we can learn a few lessons from the way dogs behave. And I think people should try harder to be dog's best friend too.

Creatures of the Night

D id you meet my Uncle Lou? Uncle Lou is tough. One of the toughest guys ever. Lives in New York. Grew up there. Says he's Brooklyn born, Brooklyn bred. When he dies, he'll be Brooklyn dead.

Uncle Lou rides the subway every day. Sometimes he works strange hours, and takes the subway very late, even middle of the night.

That's when they come out. Middle of the night. The nighttime subway menagerie, he calls 'em. Creatures of the night, he calls 'em. Everybody else calls 'em … mice and rats. Rats and mice, mice and rats. They run around on the subway tracks like they own the place, according to Uncle Lou.

Funny thing is – it doesn't bother him. Uncle Lou has a unique perspective. Says he noticed something … standing on that cold, dark, dirty subway platform … watching those creatures of the night scurrying back and forth … in and out of the shadows.

Uncle Lou tells me you'll never see mice and rats together. They never cohabitate. If you see mice, then you won't see rats. If you see rats, then you won't see mice.

Makes sense because they're two different species. Why is that important? Because we look at problems facing us in life …. and they look like they can pile up against us, even overwhelm us.

Sometimes, all we see are the problems, all those little mice and big rats running around on our subway tracks …. when we need those tracks to move forward in life.

That's how Uncle Lou explained it. *"We all have problems. But don't be overwhelmed,"* he told me. *"Instead, just be whelmed."*

Look at your problems one at a time. They showed up one at a time. You can solve them one at a time. Never let your problems all mix together in your mind. Don't let them cohabitate.

Don't be overwhelmed. Instead, just be whelmed.

An Old Family Photograph

I did something bad today. I looked at pictures that are not good for me.

No. Not what you're thinking.

I went in the closet of my parents' bedroom and took out the forbidden book. The album of my father's secret life, with all the old photographs of his first wife and child. I've done it before. Lately, I do it more and more. I don't know why. I don't even like looking at those old pictures.

Especially that photograph on the third page. Lower right corner. That happy little boy with the funny, crooked smile who looked just like me when I was his age. My father's first son ... who I never met ... and never will meet ... who looked just like me.

Dad doesn't know. Mom knows. She doesn't like it. Going back in time, she calls it. She says it's not good. It would be different if those people in the pictures were still here. But they're not. They're in the other world now, she tells me, and we're supposed to leave them alone.

Mom says it might be a sin. Because if there is such a thing as the other world, then they're busy with their own stuff. Responsibilities we can't understand from down here. We're not supposed to bother them. It might be a distraction.

That's what my mother thinks. Mom always has good ideas, good advice. I know she's just looking out for me. And I guess she's right.

Still, I can't help thinking about going back in that closet again ... to look at my big brother in that little picture.

Okay, my half big brother. Or my big half brother. My big half brother with the funny, crooked smile who I never got to meet. And never will get to meet.

Except every time I look in the closet ... and every time I look in the mirror.

Those They Left Behind

My dad always tells the story of Betty and Sally. Two sisters he went to middle school with. Prettiest girls in the whole school. Sally was in his class. Dad had a big crush on Sally. This was way before he met my mother, of course.

They were super nice. Two friendly, normal, happy girls. Everything to look forward to in life. Until one Saturday morning when their father did the unthinkable. He locked himself in the garage and started the car. Betty and Sally's father committed suicide by breathing in the gas from his own car.

They never learned why. I guess the why doesn't matter. Because it's probably one of the usual things. Money, job, health, stress, worrying about the future, or some kind of personal or family problem. Most likely one of those, right?

Everyone has some kind of major problem, even a catastrophe, at some point. But I swear … I never understood what makes a person want to take his own life. There's always an answer. There's always a way out.

Mom says suicide is a permanent solution to a temporary problem. Dad calls it the coward's way out. Because a person who makes that choice doesn't think about the effect on those they left behind.

Dad says some kids turn out great because of their parents. And sometimes … in spite of their parents.

Betty and Sally turned out just fine. Thank goodness. I don't even know how they could after what they went through. Dad saw them at his class reunion. They were happy, smart, successful, well-adjusted … totally inspiring. They must be two super strong ladies. Amazing.

And it's really a shame their father didn't stick around. He never got to see how his two beautiful baby girls turned out. How they took that awful legacy he left them with … and somehow turned it all around for their good.

He would have been so proud.

The Five Musketeers

My mom loves to tell this story. After she graduated college, she and her four best girlfriends moved down to the city. The big, bad city.

They all got their own places. They all got jobs. They were all pretty happy. Doing good things. They stayed best friends too. They called themselves The Five Musketeers.

Then one girl, Lily, had some things happen to her. All at once. She lost her job. Got kicked out of her apartment. Fiancee` broke off their engagement. And then she fell down the stairs and broke her leg. A real string of bad luck.

Lily didn't know what to do. So she gave up. She told her friends she was going back home to her mom and dad. She'll move back to the city later and try again.

My mom and the other three girlfriends took Lily out for a nice dinner to say goodbye. Over dinner they told her – *"No. You're not leaving. We're not gonna let you. You may never come back."*

Lily was surprised. She wanted to stay. But … no job, no money, no place to live … and a broken leg!

Then the other Musketeers told Lily – *"We worked it all out. Give us one year to help you get back on your feet. You'll stay with each one of us for three months. Then you'll move on to the next apartment. You'll stay on the couch. It won't cost you any money. Not even your food. Just stay with us. Please stay. Let your friends help you. We've got your back. We can do this."*

And that's what they did. Lily accepted their offer. Eventually … things got better. Her leg healed. She got a new place and found a much better job.

And you know what else ... Lily, my mother, and the other three ladies are still the best of friends ... twenty years later.

Nice story, huh? True story too. And it makes you think. Mom always tells me it's easy to recognize your real friends. Very easy. Easier than most people realize. Because a real friend walks in when the rest of the world walks out.

Mike Kimmel

It's a Little Thing

It's not fair. Math teacher does it every day. Not fair to my English teacher. My basketball coach does it, but I don't think it's fair to the team.

The school secretary does it – way too much – and her coworkers have to pick up the slack. They pick up the slack every day.

Don't know how they get away with it, but they get away with it. Been getting away with it for years.

You might say it's not a big thing. It's a little thing. Correct. Very little. About three inches long, wrapped in white paper. Roughly the size of a cigarette. Because it is a cigarette.

People go outside five, six times a day to take cigarette breaks. Just a minute or two, they say. Yeah, right. Four, five minutes is more like it. Plus a minute or two to walk out ... and then back in. Ten minutes all together. Multiplied by five or six times, and boom. You got an hour a day. A good hour. Day in, day out ... that they're not doing what they're supposed to do. They're not doing their jobs. That makes double work for everybody else.

Maybe it's not a big thing. It's a little thing. But little things add up. They add up to something that's unfair. Nobody wants to talk about this. But it's not fair. So I'm talking about it. Whether you listen is up to you.

And now, if you'll excuse me ... I really gotta go. My mom asked me to run out and pick up cigarettes. Yeah, I know, I know. This errand is taking me away from doing something else.

This little thing is taking up time I could be studying. Or exercising … or … finding something else to complain about …

But I'm working on my mom … I'm trying … and some-day I'll help her quit smoking. Someday. And someday she's gonna thank me. Just … probably not today …

The Value of a Nickel

Did I ever tell you about my Great Grandmother? My father's grandma. My Great Grandmother is amazing. Hilarious too! She says she can't *believe* how much things cost these days. Always says "these days" ... not like "those days" ... when she was my age. She can't even wrap her brain around prices nowadays.

She says nobody understands the value of a dollar any more.

Great Grandmother tells me she used to get a nickel every Saturday. That was her allowance when she was a kid.

What could you even buy with a nickel?

Great Grandmother says she was so happy to get that nickel. She could go to the store and buy a few of her favorite penny candies. Really, Great Grandmother? A penny? Yep. Some were even two for a penny!

She used to love those candies, and look forward to buying them all week long. So I ask her – *"What year was this? Who was President when you were a little girl?"*

And she says ... *"George Washington."*

Told you she's hilarious. You see, I believe a lot of people don't think older folks, senior citizens, have any sense of humor. That's because they never sit down and talk to them. Believe me, if they met my Great Grandmother, they would laugh themselves silly listening to her jokes and stories.

But that's the thing. You've gotta take time to talk and listen to people who are not just like you. And that's how you can learn from people ... understand people ... with a whole different set of experiences from your own.

People like my Great Grandmother who open up your mind to what it was like to live so long ago. People who help you appreciate all the modern conveniences we now enjoy – and usually take for granted.

And help you appreciate the value of a dollar. Even the value of a nickel.

Don't Ask Too Many Questions

Take my advice. Mind your business. Don't ask too many questions. Ask a lot of questions ... and some are gonna sound ... not so bright. You don't wanna come across as not too bright. You wanna be very bright.

When you ask the wrong question at the wrong time to the wrong person, you get an answer you won't like. Matter of fact, the answer might keep you up all night.

I'm telling you because this happened to me. With my Uncle Charlie, Dad's big brother. Everyone's favorite uncle. Nicest guy you ever met. Like a big kid. Sweet, friendly, humble.

Uncle Charlie never got married, never drank alcohol, didn't have a good job like my dad and the other brothers. Uncle Charlie never drove a car or even learned to swim. Never got in the pool. While Dad and his other brothers were swimming, having fun, drinking beers, Uncle Charlie would sit there by the pool, drinking a soda ... with his shirt buttoned up to the top. Never even put on a pair of trunks.

One sunny summer day, yours truly had the bright idea of asking Uncle Charlie why he never got in the water. Why he never learned to swim. Uncle Charlie got a funny kind of a look on his face. Then he took his shirt off ... and showed me why.

I saw the little, round, circle marks on his back and his shoulders. Dozens of them. From all the cigarettes they put out on my Uncle Charlie when he was just a boy.

Dad never told me, but Uncle Charlie showed me. He showed me good. And I learned that day not to ask so many questions.

But the question they shoulda asked was to Grandpa … who can no longer answer. Somebody shoulda asked – *"Why were you so rough on your oldest boy? Why did you do such bad things to your son Charlie?"*

My sweet old Uncle Charlie … who never bothers anybody.

Happy Birthday To Me

Today's my birthday. Happy birthday to me. We're celebrating. You're invited. Hope you'll join me. We got a seven layer chocolate cake. You can have the biggest piece. I'll cut it for you myself.

Had a wonderful time yesterday. Yesterday was my birthday. Threw a great, big party. We had elephants, magicians, ventriloquists ... and fifty-seven guys making balloon animals. Best birthday bash ever. Happy birthday to me.

Can't wait for tomorrow. Tomorrow's my birthday. I'm gonna make it special by doing something nice, something good for someone who won't even know I did it. Paying it forward, you know? Happy birthday to me.

A couple years ago, I went through a little rough patch. Honestly, it was rougher than rough. It was rough on my family too. Touch and go for a while.

But I made it. Yes, I did. Winston Churchill said, *"If you're going through hell ... keep going."* Took his advice, yes I did. That's how I made it through to the other side ... relatively unscathed.

And so ... here I stand before you today ... on my birthday. Restored, renewed, refreshed, regenerated, reinvigorated. Tall, strong, good-lookin' ... and almost completely intact.

Just missing a few little pieces. Just happy to be with you today. Not complaining about nothing anymore, I promise. Just happy to be alive. And happy to be walking around for another year ... celebrating another birthday ... on this beautiful blue marble in space that we all call home.

Grandpa – may he rest in peace – used to say something I never understood. *"I may not be where I want to be, but at least I'm not where I used to be."* I didn't understand it then, but I sure understand now.

That's why every day's my birthday. You're invited. I want you to celebrate with me. Happy birthday to me ... and to you too. Happy, happy birthday. And many, many more.

It's All About The Pizza

Gotta tell you about my brother Frankie. My brother by marriage, but that's not important. What's important is what we can learn from him.

Frankie's a true artist. He does everything with meticulous attention to detail. Skill, care, thoughtfulness. Masterful, that's what I'd call him.

His car is perfectly clean. Always dresses nice. Not expensive – just nice. Never sloppy. Always clean shaven. Good manners too. Says please and thank you. Sir and ma'am. Even finds time to send little thank you notes, hand written. Perfect handwriting. Of course.

Frankie doesn't make a lot of money, but always has enough for a little present ... a gift for someone who's feeling down. A book from the thrift store, a little stationary set, just something to make people feel appreciated. Like someone's looking out for you. Someone's got your back. Someone cares.

Everybody needs someone to look up to. I consider Frankie my role model. He inspires me to kick things up a notch, to do a little better myself.

Sometimes ... when I'm feeling low ... I swing by his job to see him. Just a minute is enough to lift me up. When he tosses that pizza dough high in the air ... oh, yeah ... it is truly a sight to behold.

Like watching a genuine artist at work. The Picasso of the pizzeria. Michaelangelo of the marinara. Also the most inspiring big brother you'd ever hope for. The Bernini of big brothers.

And Frankie is so humble too. Doesn't think he's doing anything special.

"I ain't doin' nothin'. Nothin' any other monkey can't do if I show him how. Just giving the nice people something good to eat. It's not about me. Not in any kinda way, shape, or form."

That's how Frankie says it.

"It's all about the pizza. I'm just the pizza man. Doing the best I can. Yes, sir. Yes, ma'am."

Attitude of Gratitude

My older brother gave me a book. Wasn't my birthday. Wasn't Christmas. Wasn't anything. My brother does stuff like that. I'm lucky to have him. Pretty amazing guy.

So it's no surprise the book he picked is pretty amazing. A book about gratitude. The writer tells us to develop an attitude of gratitude. I never heard anybody talk like that. I mean write like that. But you know what I mean.

Most people complain about how horrible everything is. How everything's so hard, such a struggle. Nothing ever works out the way it should. Nothing goes the way it's supposed to. People always let you down.

But that's not even true. There are always gonna be tough times. We know that. But what's important is how we handle them. And make up our minds to look for the good. And be grateful we have the opportunity and the desire to go through life that way.

And people won't always let you down. My brother's a people and he never lets me down. He never disappoints. My brother says every day is special.

But we have to find those special parts. We have to break through that wall, that hard shell so many people have built up inside. We have to find that thing that's special. Like cracking open an oyster to find that bright little pearl shining through from within. From that dark place.

That's how we've got to be. We've got to be those bright shining pearls. Bright, shining lights in a dark world. That's what an attitude of gratitude does for you.

Gratitude shines a light in the darkness. It helps you be the light in the darkness. So many people need that these days. Show gratitude everywhere you go.

When you do, you'll be doing something very, very special for this world. For this dark, scary, unpredictable, weird … and oh-so-wonderful world of ours.

That Weird Gray Zone

D id it ever occur to you that most people are living in this weird "gray zone?"

The gray zone between working and not working. Active and passive. Paying attention when you're talking, and playing on their phones when you're talking. Pretending they're listening. Listening with one ear – instead of being fully engaged. Tuning you out. Tuning the world out. That's how a lot of people go through life.

It's not only my generation. Sure, people my age might be the biggest culprits. But it's also people your age. Even kids! My little sister's age!

Everybody's living in this weird gray zone! Between paying attention and zoning out. Working and goofing off. Studying hard and doing the bare minimum. Just squeaking by. Why do they bother? What are they doing? Why are they here?

Good question. Great question. And, like a lot of great questions, it deserves a great answer. I believe I've got one. Ready? Here goes.

People are looking for someone to tell them where to go, what to do, and how to do it. People are looking for the instructions on the box.

Ironically … if you want to accomplish anything worthwhile … you've got to write your own set of instructions.

You've got to develop a sense of purpose. Set some goals. And then move towards them little by little every day. Les Brown says we must have patience and engage in consistent action. Great advice to help us get out of that weird, gray zone.

So stop looking for those instructions on the box. And start thinking outside the box.

Think outside the box, and you'll find your own instructions, your own unique, personalized roadmap to take you out of that weird, gray zone … and lead you where you really want to go in life.

The Elephant in the Room

I'm here to talk with you about the elephant in the room. "Elephant in the room" is a famous expression. An oldie but a goodie. It's something in the room – something real and definitely there – that nobody even wants to talk about.

Why? I'm glad you asked that question. Because it's uncomfortable, that's why. As a matter of fact, it's so uncomfortable people pretend it doesn't exist.

But I'm here to tell you the truth. And you can believe me or not believe me. That's up to you. Your choice. Yours and yours alone.

Ready? Here goes. We gotta kick things up a notch. All of us. We gotta work harder. We gotta do more. We gotta do more so we can have more and be more. We are absolutely not working hard enough. We're all guilty of it.

We're not working hard enough in school. Not working hard enough in sports.

Not working hard enough with our families – and in our friendships. Friendships?! Yeah, friendships take work too, believe me. And most of us aren't doing enough ... myself included.

So, I'm inviting you into new, uncharted territory. A journey of exploration and self-discovery. That's right, self-discovery. I want us to discover our true selves, our hidden selves, our real selves.

The way to find our real selves is to look for 'em. We gotta go search. That means we have to actually do something! Jack London said you can't sit around waiting for inspiration. You have to go after it with a club.

Let's make up our minds to do that. Because when we do all we're capable of ... when we become who we're supposed to be ... we're unstoppable. And unstoppable should always be the goal.

Go for unstoppable. Then you can say – *"I have met the elephant in the room ... and he is me ... no longer. And never again."*

Better Than Last Time

Practice makes …

Come on. Together now, okay? Practice makes …

No! Practice does *not* make perfect. Practice only makes us … better. Practice makes us better than the last time.

We're never gonna be perfect. So stop being so rough on yourself. Stop beating up on yourself. We've all been doing that way too long, and we have to stop doing it. Immediately. If not sooner.

A lot of people – when they want to do something new – say they won't try it unless they know they can do it right. Wrong!

Are you one of those? Are you a perfectionist? Are you the type who won't start until you can do everything perfectly the first time? Never gonna happen, my friend. That perfection train derailed a long time ago. It's not rolling back in the station anytime soon.

If you want to do something big in your life, you've got to be willing to do it wrong. You don't have to get everything right, but you have to be willing to roll up your sleeves and get it wrong.

That's where learning comes from. That's how growth takes place. It's only achieved through study and practice. Getting things wrong is how we learn, advance, and get better – in every area of our lives.

You gotta be willing to mess it up and get it wrong. That's the only way to get better.

And when we keep getting better, little by little, that's how we finally learn to get it right.

You don't have to be perfect, okay? You just have to hang in there and learn how to do things a little better than last time. A little bit is okay. All those little bits add up over time.

Time's gonna pass anyway, my friends. You might as well be productive while it does.

False. Evidence. Appearing. Real.

I've heard it said that a lot of people are afraid to be themselves. Fear holds people back from doing the things they want to do in life. And it's not just people my age. It's even people of my parents' and grandparents' generation too.

Where would we all be if Steve Jobs had been afraid nobody was going to like the cellular phones and personal computers he invented?

Where would we be if Steven Spielberg had been afraid nobody would want to see his movies?

Where would we be if John Grisham stayed inside his comfort zone? If he stuck to his safe, secure job as an attorney. The world would have never received the gift of his writing talents. We'd never have all those powerful novels. All those page-turners, exciting legal dramas that became blockbuster films with Julia Roberts, Matthew McConaughey, Denzel Washington, Matt Damon, and so many other Hollywood stars in some of the greatest roles of their careers.

But fear is internal. If you think about it, it really doesn't exist in the outside world. No such thing as fear. Fear is False Evidence Appearing Real. F.E.A.R.

You can't see it, but it's everywhere. You can't hear it, but it whispers negative thoughts in your ear. You can't taste it, but it's bitter, sour, and stale. You can't smell it ... but I think it stinks. You can't touch it, but I'd love to slap its ugly face. The ugly face of fear.

What is fear keeping you from? A new job? Playing an instrument? Writing a song, a story, or a book? Asking out that special person?

Fear may be keeping you from all these things. Fear may even be keeping you from your destiny. Going through life full of fear is insane. It's like trying to drive a car with the emergency brake on. It just won't get you where you want to go.

Don't give in to fear. Fight back. Become stronger than your fear. Make fear ... fear you.

No Turning Back

When I was little, I read a story about Vikings. Not the football team. Not the Minnesota Vikings. Vikings we learned about in World History. From hundreds of years ago. Vikings with helmets. And horns growing out on the sides. Those Vikings.

Not exactly my fashion statement of choice, but they did something that got my attention. They used to load up the ship, travel across the ocean, and touch down on a foreign shore. Then they would attack, and try to take over the whole place. I'm not praising them for that. That part's barbaric. Definitely overly aggressive. My Psych teacher would say they had an overly developed Ego. Maybe yes. Maybe no. I'm not a Viking psychologist.

But the Vikings did something we can learn from. Maybe it's a legend. Maybe not. I'm not a Viking historian. But one time they landed on a foreign shore ... and burned down their own ship.

Then their Captain said – *"Now we have to win. No turning back."*

We learned about Ulysses S. Grant in history class too. American Civil War General. General Grant said – *"Our task is to rise and continue."* I love that advice. *"Rise and continue."*

When he says – *"Rise and continue"* – that implies we've fallen. Got knocked down a peg or two. We all get knocked down from time to time. Sometimes more than from time to time. Sometimes more than a peg or two. So when something's not working, not going your way ... think about the Vikings. Think about General Grant. Ask yourself what they'd do.

What's important is not that we get knocked down – but how long we decide to stay down. Think about those Vikings and General Grant. They wouldn't stay down long.

Let's be more like those guys. No matter what happens to us. *"Rise and continue. No turning back."*

Lessons I've Learned

Have you ever wanted something so badly you can taste it? Something that's so important ... nothing else matters? Yeah, me too.

In life, you're either winning or learning. A lot of people think it's winning or losing, but that's not exactly right. Not exactly. Because, if something doesn't go your way ... yes, you've lost, but ask yourself what else is going on in that situation?

My favorite teacher always asks us: *"Where's the lesson? What can we learn from this? What's our take-away?"*

And there's always a lesson to be learned. Because we're always changing, always growing, always evolving.

This is not up for debate. Because we're always in motion. Our bodies and our minds are always in motion. And by being in motion, we're going to come up against some stuff.

We will have challenges. We will have obstacles. And when we run up against them, we will either win ... or we won't win.

Yes, sometimes in life we're going to fail. There. I said it. I don't like that word, but I said it. The F word. Failure. People spend their whole lives running from it, in fear of it. But they shouldn't. Failure is not fatal, and failure is not final.

Failure is an open door, not a closed door. Failure is an opportunity to put on our thinking caps and strategize. We learn something when we fail in life. We learn something when we get disappointed, when something doesn't go our way, and when people let us down.

We're gonna get knocked down sometimes. What's important is not how often we get knocked down, but how quickly we get back up.

So ... when you get knocked down, what do you do? Push-ups! That's what you do. Learn something from every setback. Learn your lesson. Grit your teeth. And do some push-ups.

Getting the Band Together

I was watching this show with my parents last night. A documentary on the Beatles. Mom and Dad *love* the Beatles. They say the Beatles were the greatest band of all time.

Yeah, I know. Just their opinion, but think about it. Fifty, sixty years later, and we're still talking about the Beatles. How many other bands got together – and have come and gone – since then? I wonder.

So the reporter was interviewing one of the Beatles – Paul McCartney. Asked him how the Beatles first got together. Because they were a garage band, you know? They were high school kids, teenagers, playing in the garage in Liverpool, England, where they're from.

And the filmmaker wanted to know how they did it, how they all got together in the first place.

Paul McCartney wasn't giving him the answers he wanted. So the reporter guy kept asking the same question in a different way. Over and over and over again. Kind of annoying, actually. How did the four of you get together? How did you start the Beatles?

And Paul finally got a little frustrated, but he said something pretty profound. *"Nobody knows how to start a band. You just get together and start playing."*

I love that answer! I told my parents that's the answer ... to everything. Anything you want to do ...nobody *really* knows how to do it, not a hundred per cent, so you just ... start playing. You get started. Put one foot in front of the other and right away ... you're moving forward. Even if it's baby steps, they're still steps. You're making progress.

That's the secret. Baby steps are okay.

That's how you do something when you don't know how. When you don't even know where to begin. When you're confused, when you're afraid, and you don't know how to get started.

You take those baby steps. You just start playing.

Put On Your Happy Face

Q uestion. Do you ever look at people's faces? I mean really look. I mean look good and hard, almost like you're a scientist, trying to discover something.

And I'm not talking about whether a person is good-looking or not. That's genetics. Something we don't have any control over. I'm talking about our actions, our attitudes. You might say our attitudes are more important than genetics. Our attitudes determine how we make use of our genetics, how we make the most of what nature gave us.

At this point, you might be saying – *"Huh?"*

You may be wondering where I'm going. Well, I'm not going. I'm staying. I'm staying with this until you get it. Because this is important. Our faces are important. We gotta put our best face forward. And there's a lot of people out there wearing a permanent scowl on their faces. Don't let that be you.

My Grandma Mollie always says – *"You've got to turn that frown upside down."*

And I know that's easier said than done. Because it's easy to put on your happy face when things are going your way. Easy to put on a happy face when your family's all getting along great. When you're getting good grades in school. When your friends are acting normal.

Unfortunately, life isn't always that way. Not for any of us. Things are gonna happen. We're gonna get knocked down a time or two. That's part of being human. But it's not about how often we get knocked down. It's about how long we allow ourselves to stay down. And the attitude we have when we get back up.

Remember – put on your happy face when you leave the house today. Yes, you! That's right. I'm talking to you!

Happiness is not random. It doesn't depend on your circumstances. Happiness is an intellectual choice. Happiness is a daily decision you make. A smile will always improve your face value.

The Consequences

Consequences. There are consequences to all our actions. Every single one. Consequences for everything we do and everything we don't do.

For every action, there's an equal but opposite reaction. I'm not trying to beat up on anybody. Really, I'm not. But some of us have been beating up on ourselves. We go through life beating up on ourselves for the actions we take each and every day.

It was Emerson who told us that the ancestor of every action is a thought. Action and thought. We're responsible for both. Through our thoughts and actions we create habits for ourselves. And it's those habits that determine the course of our days ... and ultimately the course of our lives.

Good habits are the result of creative thinking, careful planning, and positive actions. Good habits bring us beneficial results. Bad habits, though, are developed through poor planning, failure to take responsibility, and inaction.

Yes, inaction. Inactivity is just as bad as taking negative actions – doing all kinds of things we know in our hearts to be wrong.

So decide. Make a good decision today. A positive choice. Realize it's all up to you. Think twice before you cheat on that test. Think twice before you make that sarcastic remark. Think twice before you reach for that eleventh candy bar.

Our actions are not up to fate. Not up to chance. If it's to be, it's up to me. It's up to me. It's up to you. It's up to all of us. So take responsibility, folks.

Take responsibility for all your thoughts, all your actions, and therefore … all your consequences. We can make decisions that bring about the right consequences, the kind of good consequences we all want for ourselves.

Those are the best kind of consequences.

I Love That Show!

Before I was born – before you were born – there was a show called *I Love Lucy*. It's still popular all over the world, even after all these years.

I discovered it when I was little, flipping channels. Soon, I was hooked. I'm still hooked. I like the show so much ... I got a book about it from the library. Yes, the library.

The show was about a married couple. Lucy, of course, was the star. Desi played her husband. Actually, he was her husband in real life too. Married on the show. Married in real life.

They were also the producers. That's another story in itself, by the way. But this book tells about something Desi did during the casting process.

You see, Desi was the creative genius behind the scenes. Very smart businessman. They were casting the show. Looking for two actors to play the neighbors, Fred and Ethel.

Ethel was fine. They found a good Ethel. Fred was the problem. They couldn't decide on a Fred. Desi actually found a Fred he liked ... but nobody agreed! Nobody else liked him. Everyone said he was too old.

But Desi stood his ground. Trusted his instincts. Went with his gut. The more people said he was wrong ... the more he knew he was right.

Desi was right ... and proved all his critics wrong. Fifty, sixty years later, their show is still great. Their show still holds up. Watch *I Love Lucy* today, and you can't imagine anyone else playing the role of Fred Mertz... except Mister William Frawley.

Seriously.

Look him up. He was terrific. But nobody would look him up ... if Desi didn't hook him up.

So think about *I Love Lucy* when everybody tells you you're wrong. And imagine what you can do if you're strong enough to trust yourself, strong enough to trust your instincts, strong enough to stand your ground.

My Deep, Dark Secret

Can you keep a secret?

I have a deep, dark secret. I don't know if I should tell you. You might want to throw me out of here. They might even kick me out of this business entirely. Career could be toast if this ever gets out.

But it's a terrible secret for an artist to bear alone. It's high time I went public. Consequences be damned.

Here goes. I'm pretty normal.

I'm a normal well-adjusted teenager. That's my secret. I don't hate my mother. I don't hate my father. In fact, I love them. I think the world of them. If anything, I feel guilty that I can never fully repay them for all their sacrifices, for everything they've done for me.

I love my little brother and sister too. I watch them when my folks are away. I teach them to ride their bikes. I help them with their homework. I would do anything for them. I would do anything for my family – and my friends too. I've got great friends.

And I'm not bragging, but I really do try my best. I respect my elders. I eat my vegetables. I don't smoke. I return my library books on time.

I'm not sarcastic. I'm not cliquish. I'm not edgy. No tattoos, no piercings. Not that there's anything wrong with that ... because I'm not judgmental, either.

But I need your help. They tell me I'm an under-represented minority, an endangered species in show business, in the acting community. So please do me this one favor. Don't tell anyone we had this conversation. This conversation never happened. Cool? Please keep my secret safe.

I hope you don't mind my sharing this burden with you. Thank you for listening.

Uh …my parents always tell me to say please and thank you. I hope that's okay.

Alligator Stew

Pardon me. Did you eat today? That's a loaded question. Loaded with possibilities. What do you like to eat? Mostly normal stuff, right? Anything weird, though? Anything out of the ordinary?

I'm not trying to be nosy ... but I'm gonna be nosy! Because I'm trying to understand something. It seems like people in different parts of the world – even different parts of our own country – eat some pretty weird foods.

I know, I know, my mom always tells me not to judge people. We don't want people judging us, either.

But we were on vacation and I saw something on a menu that kinda freaked me out. Freaked. Me. Out. The special of the day was ... are you ready? Alligator stew! Blech! Nasty!

Okay ... I guess I'm judging now.

Because it's what you're comfortable with, right? Generally, I'm a lot more comfortable with cheeseburgers than alligators, but that's just me. That's not you. And that's okay. Because maybe in some weird, parallel universe – there I am, begging my mom to cook us up a big old pot of alligator stew for din-din. I don't particularly think that's the case, but who can say for sure?

I just can't believe I can get on board for alligator stew ... in this or any other parallel universe. Maybe in a perpendicular universe, but not any kind of parallel one.

But like I said, I'm trying. Trying to understand. And not judge. So I asked our waiter – not in a challenging way – what does alligator stew even taste like?

He says it tastes just like chicken.

No way. Crazy, right? I'm not buying that old story. They always say that. They say everything tastes like chicken.

But … I've got a funny feeling alligator tastes a lot more like … crocodile.

Mike Kimmel

Do I Smell?

Do you smell something funny? Let me rephrase that. Do I smell a little funky to you?

No, really. Do you think I smell bad? I never noticed, but you can't tell for sure, right? You can tell with other people, but not always yourself.

I'm only asking because something funny happened. Not ha-ha funny, but weird funny.

I got a birthday present from my aunt and uncle in a really nice box. I thought it would be a nice present. Some cool clothes, sharp looking shoes, maybe a new phone. A video game – or a new game system – would be all right. Or cash. I wouldn't mind cash, so I can buy whatever I want. Not a bad option.

You know what was in the box? A nice, big bottle of body wash. Yes. Body wash. Really? Is this a hint? Like offering someone a breath mint? Are they trying to tell me something?

My aunt and uncle are super nice people. Always liked them. And my folks tell us to respect our elders. I totally get that. They're great people. But ... body wash?! Nice birthday present – telling someone they stink!

So I'm asking again. You won't hurt my feelings. Do I smell a little funky to you?

Okay, you're not saying anything ... so I'm not sure how to take that. If you don't respond, it means ... you're thinking – *"Yes"* – but don't want to say anything to hurt my feelings. Is that what you're telling me? With your silence, I mean.

58

Sometimes, what a person doesn't say speaks louder than what he says out loud. Or what she says out loud. Am I reading your non-verbal response correctly?

Uh … all right … this is getting the tiniest bit uncomfortable now. Maybe I better leave. Yes, I am gonna leave.

Thank you for your time. You can exhale now.

First Car

I think it's time. Time for me to join the team, join that exclusive and prestigious club.

I am ready. Got all my paperwork done. Documented and confirmed. And now I'm ready to take part, to make my mark, and to finally get myself out on the open road.

I feel ready too. I was top student in my Driver's Ed class. Some of my classmates, unfortunately, are a little more ... apprehensive ... about participating in the motor vehicle operating activities ... for which we have now been fully trained. They don't quite feel ready to step up and enter the fray.

One of them even asked if he could drive on the sidewalk. At least for a little while until he feels more comfortable. Says he doesn't wanna be out in the street with all those crazy drivers.

But sometimes, you just have to learn to trust yourself. Trust builds self-confidence. Maybe I trust myself too much. But I think most people trust themselves too little ... or don't trust themselves at all. That's why I asked Mom and Dad for a new car. Not some little junk job, either.

My dad says his first car was a Rolls. Not a Rolls Royce. A Rolls Canardly. Ever hear of the old Classic Rolls Canardly? Rolls down one hill. Can hardly make it up the next. That's not gonna work for me.

No, no, no, no, no. I'm setting my sights a little higher. I'm driving a Rolls Royce. I'm driving a Bentley. My folks say I'm driving them crazy.

But some days that's a pretty short trip.

And I'm setting my sights higher. Higher, ladies and gentlemen. Long trips. Maybe cross country. Maybe even all over the world. No half measures. No way, no how. No short trips for me. No, sir.

No Rolls Canardly.

Little Green Men

Question of the day. You might not want to answer, and that's okay. It's personal, and the answer will be different for every person.

Tell me. What would you say to a guy ... from ... another planet? Seriously. If a space ship landed – right here outside – and a little green man popped out ... then what? Pretty significant event, right? What would be your response to that event? What would you say? What would you do?

He doesn't have to be green. Doesn't even have to be a man. Or little. How about a big, honkin', scary-looking alien? Who comes down here to get us, just like in that movie?

What would be your natural response? Would you walk up to that space ship with an open hand or a closed fist? Both responses might be equally valid, equally appropriate given all of our personal differences. Your reaction might be very different from mine. From the lady down the hall. From my Uncle Charlie.

That's okay. Because I hear people on TV. They say we're a divided people, a divided nation. Young and old, left and right, Democrats and Republicans. When you get right down to it, though, don't we need both sides? That's positive, not negative. Together, we're the yin and the yang.

So I say to you – what keeps us apart? What's keeping us divided when we can be united? Let's celebrate our diversity today. Not just diversity of color, of religion, nationality, income levels – but our diversity of opinion, as well. That's a part of who we are as a species on planet Earth.

I invite you to embrace your inner Earthling today. We have more things in common than things that separate us. It's time we all embraced our inner Earthling. Let's get ourselves together – and keep ourselves together – as a people and as a planet.

I'm Not a Morning Person

Gotta admit. I'm not a morning person. Especially Monday mornings. I like to go out on the weekends and have fun. I'm not a *real* big party animal like some of my friends. Some of them never stop. Go, go go, every weekend. Rain, snow, or shine.

But me and mornings ... have never been on the best of terms. And Monday mornings are the toughest. It's like my Uncle Adam says. The first five days after the weekend are always the hardest. He's not a morning person, either ... as you may have guessed.

Dad's definitely a morning person. He wakes up at four o'clock to hit the gym for an hour before work. Honestly, I wish I could be more like him. I turned out more like Mom. She says she likes to get up at the crack of noon. Mom's pretty funny. But she *will sleep* till noon if we let her. Mostly on weekends. She can't get away with that during the week, but on Saturday and Sunday she hibernates like a grizzly bear.

Dad calls her Grizzly Mom. He used to call her his Sleepy Little Polar Bear, but she didn't like that much. Said it made her sound coldhearted. Not sure Grizzly Mom is any more endearing, though.

But Mom and Dad always seem to figure it out. They get along great. Better than any of my friends' parents. Just shows ... you don't have to be with somebody who's your mirror image. A little variety is nice.

Mom says in any relationship where two people agree on everything ... one of them is unnecessary.

So maybe it's true that opposites attract. Or maybe my mother and father are just two awesome human beings. Two smart, good-natured people who don't let stupid little things come between them ... like who's a morning person and who's not.

The Other Side of Fifty

My mother just celebrated a milestone.. Had a milestone birthday last weekend. Hit the big five-o. Yep, fifty years old this past Sunday. And she's not taking it well, I can tell you that right now.

Mom keeps asking – *"How did I get over the hill without reaching the top?"*

But Dad doesn't like her talking like that. So he interrupts. He says he's not letting his favorite leading lady off the hook. Dad says there's no room in his house for what he calls negative self-talk. That kind of mess is strictly forbidden. And he means it too. He's always calling me out when he catches me running my mouth, putting myself down … even when I'm just joking around.

Yeah, Dad doesn't like those kind of put-downs. Calls it stinkin' thinkin'. I love that expression, because we're all guilty from time to time. And Dad says we gotta chase that stinkin' thinkin' out of our heads before it takes root.

Then he told Mom she's not really fifty. She's actually two twenty-five year olds.

Then he kinda looked her up and down and growled. Yeah, I said growled. Real flirty. Like they're still in high school.

So Mom gives him a look. She knows she doesn't look like she did when she was twenty-five. But I know she still likes it when Dad says stuff like that.

My father's kind of a wildman. You mighta figured that out already. Definitely an optimist. Mom says he's the greatest optimist in the world. Number one optimist. Optimist Prime.

But maybe he's gotta be to compensate for all the pessimists out there in this world.

Some people find all that sunshine a little annoying. Sometimes I do too. I admit it. But ... you know what? I hope I can be more like my dad when I get to the other side of fifty.

Allergic to Average

I'm allergic. Lotta people got allergies nowadays. My grandfather has an interesting perspective. Grandpa says nobody even had allergies when he was my age.

But something's in the air now that's ... different from previous generations.

Can you guess? Know what I'm allergic to? Hint. It's all around. Nope. Not pollen, dillweed, ragweed, or seaweed. Something harder to avoid. No, not nuts. I mean I'm ... not allergic to nuts and I'm ... not nuts myself. No, not dairy. Not soy. Give up?

I'm allergic to something there's no vaccination for!

Allergic to average! I can't stand average. I'd rather fall on my face. I'd rather fail outright – than just be average.

Grandpa says average is the best of the worst and the worst of the best. I think he's right. Nowadays, people make so many excuses. Excuses for not doing what they're supposed to do. Not doing what they know they should.

When he was a teenager, Grandpa worked two jobs and went to school at night. If I have basketball practice and SAT class on the same day I need a nap. What's wrong with my generation? We should be getting stronger, better, smarter, more disciplined. Not the other way around.

Do you think we may have lost something?

They call Grandpa's generation *The Greatest Generation*. What are they gonna call our generation? *The Crybaby Generation? The Excuse-Making Generation?*

Maybe ... *Just Another Average Generation?*

Those titles are not too complimentary. Maybe we've become complacent. Maybe we've become comfortable being just another average generation. But we don't have to stay that way.

And I'm definitely not staying that way. I want to live Grandpa's way. Like back in the day. Because I'm allergic to average.

One-Dollar Sunglasses

I'd like to share something. I never get compliments on my sunglasses. That's okay. I didn't get them for other people. I got them for me. I'm the one who's gotta like 'em or not like 'em.

I like 'em just fine. Know what I like most? The price. Got 'em at my favorite store. Old reliable. The dollar store. Where you can really stretch your dollar. And I like to stretch my dollar until it screams for mercy.

Enough about me. We have come to the audience participation portion of our program. Tell me. What's the number one reason to replace sunglasses?

Correct! You lost them. Sunglasses. Umbrellas. Am I right or am I right?

Do you see where I'm going? Stay with me. The best thing about buying cheap sunglasses is when you forget them somewhere ... they're still there when you go back. Nobody wants them so nobody steals them. Nobody's looking for a five-finger discount. Nobody wants my sunglasses except me.

Fine. The person who bought them wants them. Because they represent something more important than a couple of flimsy pieces of plastic to guard my eyes from the sun. Which they do reasonably well, by the way.

They represent credibility and validation. Proof I know what I'm doing. I know my way around. I'm nobody's fool. Nobody's sap. Nobody's human sock puppet.

Grandpa says the more you know, the less you need. I don't need to impress anybody ... especially people who are impressed by designer clothes ... and shoes ... and sunglasses.

So like me *for me*. Or *don't* like me for me. And if you like me for me, your reason can be … I'm comfortable in my own skin. I may not have everything figured out, but I'm confident enough … to prefer practicality over style.

And that's my style. One-dollar sunglasses style.

First Day of Work

Did you ever go to the circus? Good. Me too. Did you see those high wire acts? I mean those people walking way up in the air ... on that tightrope ... with the long bar to help balance. How does someone start walking the tightrope? How does someone learn that? How do they begin?

I get it. There's a teacher, trainer, mentor. An experienced circus performer. With someone training you, you get better and better. No surprises there. But what about the very first time? What's the first day like? What's Your Day One Tightrope Walking Experience consist of?

How does somebody do it the very first time? There has to be a first time, doesn't there? Explain to me the first day on the job. That's what I want to know about.

Someone said it doesn't matter what you do ... as long as you get started. But how do you start a hundred feet up in the air? One wrong move and the day you start is the day you finish. First day equals last day.

And what about other dangerous jobs? What about those guys who go in the water and wrestle alligators? How do they get started? I know, someone trains them too. But how do they train? Does the Professional Reptile Wrestling Coach send them in the pool to practice with inflatable alligators? What's *their* first day like? What's their next step after that?

I'm curious because my brother started a new job after school. He's working at a restaurant. And he gets all stressed out because there are so many new things to learn.

But at least he's learning with both feet on the ground. Not way up in the air ... and not down in the water surrounded by alligators. Much better learning environment if you ask me. Much easier first day of work.

Do Candy Bars Talk To You?

Do candy bars talk to you? Or just me? I'm serious, they speak to me. Mostly chocolate bars. When I walk by the machine, they say stuff. Not in a bad way. They're not rude. They're actually pretty funny. The stuff they say is funny too. *"Hey you! Come here! Stop what you're doing. Stay a while, why don't ya? I got something good for you."* Stuff like that. It grabs your attention when you're a busy teenager.

And if they're going to all that trouble to seek me out … connect on a personal basis … who am I not to answer them?

Ever since I was little, candy bars have been my favorite food. I like other stuff too. But candy bars are the best, no question about it. Best of the best, no time for the rest.

So, if you need someone for a candy bar eating contest, I am your candidate. I'll get the job done. Eat so many, I'll get corporate sponsorship for our school. Like famous athletes with company names printed on their sweat suits. That will be me. Companies will line up to donate money. Because when it comes to candy bars, milk chocolate, dark chocolate, with nuts, without nuts, caramel, no caramel … I am a juggernaut, unstoppable, in a class by myself.

I can eat more of those things than any human being on this planet.

I'm a busy teenager. Got a lot on my plate. But there's always room on that plate for a nice candy bar. Or two. Let's be real … three candy bars. Maybe even king size. Because, for me, chocolate is not just a delicious treat, it's a way of life.

Candy bars speak to me … and that's why I'm speaking to you.

Will You Take This Brief Survey?

There's this new store in the mall, right? Well, no ... I'm not asking you if there's a new store. I know there's a new store, because I went there yesterday. Little stationary shop with cards, notebooks, markers, things like that.

They're having a grand opening sale. So I figured, what the heck? I'll go in. Pretty nice place, pretty good sale, some cool pens, notebooks ... nice stuff. So I bought a couple of things. I figured I'm here anyway ... what the heck?

That was yesterday.

Today I get a phone call from the store. Some kinda survey. Huh? Asking me all kinds of questions. How nice the store looked. How friendly the employees were. How long I had to wait. Can I rate their customer service?

What the heck?!

Why are they calling and bothering their customers?! Then they ask the big question. Would I recommend their store to others?! Would I?! No, I wouldn't recommend the store to others! Not now, I wouldn't! Maybe yesterday. Now I wouldn't even recommend the store to myself! Maybe before, but not now! Not after they start calling me, bothering me with stupid surveys. Now I won't even recommend your store to me!

My mother says I'm overreacting. I say I'm under-reacting! She says the store's just trying to be nice. Yeah, well, maybe they should try a little harder, because what they're doing to be nice is not working. Not with me, anyway.

So, let's be clear, Mr. and Mrs. New Stationary Shop Owners in the mall. No. No, I will not take this brief survey.

No, I will not recommend your store to my family and close friends. And no, I will definitely not return. Please delete my number. Email address too.

And take me off your Christmas card list, please. You have lost my business forever.

P.S. I'm unfriending you.

The High Cost of Mailing

My father got mad today. Not at me. At the Post Office. Yeah, I know. Sometimes Dad gets mad too easily. But he's right about this one.

Seriously. Why is it so expensive to mail stuff? Why do they keep raising the price of stamps? Seems like they go up every year. Every two years.

I have an idea. Instead of raising the price of those adorable little square stamps we all know and love so much ... how about making them smaller? That way it wouldn't cost so much to print them and the Post Office wouldn't have to raise the price every year.

You like that?

Good, because I've got another one. You know all those pictures they put on the stamps? We bought stamps with pictures of winter wonderland scenes. Kids on sleds, reindeer frolicking through the forest, squirrels hiding the chestnuts, woodpeckers. Seriously?

Last year they had stamps with famous cartoon characters. If I want to watch cartoons, I'll turn on the TV. I don't have to mail a letter for that.

Sure, it's nice to have pictures of our favorite cartoons, and kids on sleds, and squirrels and chipmunks. But they have to pay an artist and designer every time they put out a new series of stamps. Who do you think they pass that cost on to? Correct!

So how about implementing a new strategy for our beloved Post Office? Two different pictures on our stamps. One – the flag. Two – the first President. You cool with that?

All right … you want to mail a letter internationally? Fine. Albert Einstein, okay? Cool? Stick Albert Einstein on your envelope. Boom, you're good to go.

And there you have it. That's how we stop the Post Office from raising their prices every year. Stop putting new pictures on the stamps and start making those stamps smaller.

Boom. Done.

Do Not Eat

Word to the wise: You know those little white plastic packets? Those little, annoying things. Silica gel packets, they're called. They put them everywhere. They're all over the place. They're in packets of beef jerky. They're in bottles of vitamins. They're in the pockets of some new clothes I bought! What the heck are those things?

Glad you asked. Because nobody knows what they are. Or what they're for. Okay, I can live with that. I don't have to understand everything. I'm not ... overly obsessive that way.

But the weirdest thing – even weirder than the fact that these bizarre little whatchamacallits even exist – is what's printed on them. *"Do not eat."*

All righty, then. Good advice for all of us. Do not eat the silica gel packets you'll find inside that new pair of shoes. Thank you. Thank you, Mr. and Mrs. Silica Gel Packet Manufacturer. Thank you for clearing that one up.

Because I was looking at that tasty little morsel you so graciously included in my recent purchase ... and was about to grab my knife and fork. So glad you stopped me!

Do not eat. Sure. Do not eat the silica gel packets. And, uh ... exactly how stupid do you think we all are? Never mind. Don't answer that. It was strictly a rhetorical question.

All this talking is making me thirsty. Maybe I'll grab a tasty beverage instead. Think I'll go down to Dad's car and pop the hood.

Oh dear! Dear me! There are warning signs there too! *"Do not drink."*

Really?

"Do not drink from car battery. Do not drink from radiator." Whew! Thank you again! I know a piping hot glass of radiator fluid – or battery acid – might seem pretty tempting to thirsty people! Thanks for the save!

Man! So many restrictions on what we can eat and drink! Guess I'll just have to wait for dinner …

Mike Kimmel

Getting in Shape

I know kids who get doctors' notes to be excused from gym class. Excused from gym class! Crazy, right? And craziest of all is that the kids who need gym the most are the ones asking for the excuses!

Excused?! These kids should be volunteering for more gym classes. They should be doubling up on gym, taking gym for extra credit!

I'm not trying to be rude. This is tough love. That's all.

There's a reason I'm tough on these kids. Full disclosure. I was one of them. I struggled with my weight for years – until I finally made up my mind to get that area of my life under control.

Back then, all I thought about was my next cheeseburger. What they were serving in the cafeteria. What goodies my mom might prepare for dessert. I used to live to eat, not eat to live. My waistline showed it. My blood type was Ragu. Back then, I would have loved to get my chubby little hands on a doctor's note to excuse me from gym. But that's the last thing I needed.

What I needed was tough love. The kind I'm dishing out. I needed someone to encourage me to eat more fruits and vegetables. Do more exercise. I've still got a ways to go. I'm not where I want to be. I want to knock off a few more pounds.

What the biggest room in the world? The room for improvement. You know what the smallest room in the world is, right? A mushroom. We should all eat more mushrooms, by the way. Very healthy.

People always talk about getting back in shape. Is it possible to get back in shape if you've never actually been in shape? No response necessary. Rhetorical question.

More tough love.

And now, if you'll excuse me, I must be off. As the sun sets slowly in the west, I bid you all a fond farewell. I have an appointment to keep with Mister Treadmill.

Mastering Procrastination

Oh good. Glad you're here. Because we really do need to talk about procrastination.

I was planning to bring this up yesterday, but I put it off. Just kidding!

Seriously – you know what the secret is to mastering procrastination? No? Okay, I'll tell you tomorrow. Joking! Honestly, though, it's not something to joke about. Procrastination is serious. I actually bought a book on procrastination, but I haven't gotten around to reading it yet.

Okay. No more jokes. Here's the answer. Never say *next time*. No such thing as *next time*. Eliminate that phrase from your vocabulary. This time is last time's next time.

So, "next time" you want to put something off – remember what Horace Greeley said.

"The way to do anything is to begin."

Great advice. To do anything, you have to actually get started. Got it? Good. Step One is to get into action.

Now – Step Two is to break the task down into smaller steps.

You know the old joke? How do you eat an elephant? One bite at a time. Step Two is to break the job down into incremental steps. Baby steps are okay. That's so it's not overwhelming for you.

And Step Three is to repeat the process. Do it all over again. This way, you get yourself into action … break the job down into smaller parts … and then repeat the process until it becomes a habit.

Wash. Rinse. Repeat.

Wash. Rinse. Repeat.

You can do this, I promise. That's how you overcome procrastination. You get started. Do a little at a time. And repeat the process until it becomes a habit.

Get it? Got it? Good. No more procrastination. We're performing an assassination on procrastination.

Gotcha. That's another joke. Last one. Now get out of here and go get started.

I Think I Had a Job Interview

I had a job interview. At least I think I did. Filled out the application. That part was fine.

Then the manager comes out. Walks me into his office. He's rather a … large …man. With thick glasses. Looks familiar. I've seen him somewhere! Maybe on TV?

Can't place him. Not yet. And it's starting to bother me. Where do I know him from? Reminds me of somebody … and … not exactly a handsome somebody.

Don't get me wrong. I'm sure he's nice. A good manager. Probably a family guy. With kids my age, a wife who loves him … and who knows how to cook a nice pot roast on his birthday. You know, to celebrate his being a responsible manager kind of a man, and holding down a good job so they can have a house, couple of freckled-face kids … and a nice pot roast whenever they want.

He sits down, starts talking … about the job, hours, responsibilities, my school schedule, and my application. Blah, blah, blah. And then more blah, blah, blah. Meanwhile, I can't pay attention, because I'm thinking … *"Where do I know this guy from?"*

Then it hits me! He looks exactly like the father on that cartoon. With the kid who has a big, funny shaped head … like a football.

Then he asks – *"Do you have any questions for me?"* And I go blank. Completely blank. He asks again. I still can't think of anything. So he asks if I'm feeling okay … then asks a third time if I have questions.

So I ask – *"How do you find a hat to fit your little boy's big, giant, football shaped head?"* I was nervous. It was all I could think of.

He gives me a funny look. Then a long pause. And says they'll let me know.

Okay. Probably not my best interview, but if he says they'll let me know … that's encouraging, right? That means I'm still in the game. That's something, anyway.

Right? Uh … right?

85

The Ugly Hats

My grandma sent me a present – these ugly hats. My grandma is a really wonderful lady. My mom's mom. Probably one of my favorite people on this whole, entire planet. But as wonderful as she is … that's how ugly these hats were.

And I didn't know what to do. Because I don't want to complain. I don't want to sound ungrateful. I love my grandmother.

But I … don't really love her taste in hats. There were two of these hats. They were plaid. Weird colors too. And … just plain ugly. I don't know where she bought them. Maybe the Ugly Hat Store?

So I felt like I had a dilemma. I was on the horns of a dilemma. Actually, if these hats had horns, they wouldn't be so ugly. Then they'd be like plaid Viking kind of helmet-hats, and I could wear them when I'm playing video games.

But I didn't want to insult my grandmother. And I definitely didn't want to wear these two … disgustingly ugly hats. So what could I do? How do I handle this … still be cool … not embarrass myself … and not disrespect my grandmother?

Then I came up with a solution. Know what I did? I made all my friends buy ugly hats too. I got all these ugly invitations from the dollar store, and I invited all my friends to join me for an Ugly Hat Party.

We all had a blast. So much fun. We took a million goofy pictures. I sent the pictures to my grandmother too. She loved them. She was so flattered.

Grandma didn't even realize I didn't like those hats! So I think this was the perfect solution. Because I love my grandmother much more than I hate those hats.

But just for the record … I have to tell you … they were really ugly hats.

The Meaning of Life

Did you ever stop and really think? I mean stop all your buzz of activity, *all your busy work*, and think long and hard about the bigger questions of our lives.

Why are we here? Kids, teenagers, even adults. I mean, why are we on this funny little planet anyway? Running to and fro … competing for grades, honors, money, dates? What is the meaning of life? Why are we here?

My older sister says we're here to serve humanity. We're here to help others. Okay. Well, then … why are the others here?

Seriously. I mean I've got kids in my class who never do anything. Just take up desk space. They never study. They never participate. What are they doing? Why are they here?

My study partner says if you put their brain inside a gold-fish, the fish would swim backwards! I know, I know. That's not nice.

So maybe these are the ones we're supposed to help. But how? I don't know. Your guess is as good as mine.

Everybody needs something. That something is different for every one of us. Kids, teens, adults. Everybody.

Maybe that's our "why." Maybe that's what we're supposed to do. Maybe that's what we're all here for ... scrambling around on Planet Earth … to figure out what the world needs and contribute something valuable to the mix.

What I need is different from what you need, different from what my dad needs, different from what that kid in math class – who never contributes – needs.

And if I've totally confused you … please understand these are the exact same questions that have baffled human beings for thousands of years. That's a good thing. If you're confused, it makes you human. A human being with human problems and human questions.

Congratulations. And welcome to Earth. Third rock from the sun.

The Chair Boy

There was an old time film director named Cecil B. DeMille. This was back in the old days. Black and white movies. Silent movies.

He was famous for doing these grand, sweeping Biblical epics. Gigantic productions, with huge open spaces, armies circling around each other in the desert, horses, chariots, pyramids. Stuff like that.

And what he would do is … walk all around … figure out the shot he wanted … the perfect camera angle … and then just sit down!

Wherever he stopped – wherever he thought he could get the best shot – that's where he sat down!

How did he do it? Funny you should ask! There was a kid. A seventeen year-old boy whose job it was to follow the director around with a chair.

You see where I'm going with this? He followed Cecil B. DeMille with a director's chair. You know, one of those wooden folding chairs with the canvas seat, canvas back.

Wherever Mr. DeMille would move, this kid had to keep up. Wherever Mr. DeMille would stop, this kid – about my age – had to be right there. He had to stuff that chair underneath this famous director's … you know what … when he finally sat down to direct the movie. Wherever the director sat … that chair better be there!

What if it wasn't? I don't know. Guess there would be a new seventeen year-old boy working that job the next day. Maybe an eighteen year-old boy. Maybe the studio would have to upgrade. Who knows?

But when I heard this story, I said – *"I'm not complaining about my little after-school job at the store ever again!"*

Think about it! What a weird job for a teenager! To follow a famous movie director around and stick a chair underneath his ... you know what!

Seriously! Some jobs are just not worth their salary!

The Easiest Thing in the World

The easiest thing in the world is to underperform. The easiest thing in the world is to do less than we're capable of doing. Just coasting. Just enough to squeak by in life.

But that's really not the way nature made us. We were made for increase, for advancement. We were meant to achieve, to excel, to make our mark, to do more than anything we could ever begin to imagine.

But so many people take the easy way, that familiar path of least resistance. Wrong approach. John F. Kennedy said we shouldn't do something because it's easy. We should do something because it's difficult. We should do the things that challenge us ... that push us to go to that next level. That's the way to grow, to evolve, to become all that we can be.

And it may not be comfortable for us. But that's okay. Growth is always uncomfortable.

The obvious example, of course, is the caterpillar that turns into a beautiful butterfly. Everyone focuses on the butterfly, but if you think about it ... that caterpillar probably made itself pretty uncomfortable though the process of growing, building, developing those strong, beautiful wings – and ultimately taking flight. That caterpillar had to go through some stuff. We should focus on the caterpillar.

So embrace your own inner caterpillar. Start today. Step out of your comfort zone.

Find that thing that's difficult for you to do and attack it. Crush it. Because doing something difficult is the easiest way in this world to build your own set of strong wings ... and take flight and soar ... like nature meant for you to do.

Magnanimity

Excuse me, but I have to say a dirty word.

Magnanimity.

Do you know what that means? Don't worry, I didn't either. It means ... selflessness. Not just being focused on you.

It's not really a dirty word, of course, but it almost seems like a dirty word these days. Because everyone out there nowadays is so *completely* focused on themselves.

Me. Me. Me. It's the Me Generation. All about me.

What's in it for me? How do I get myself out there ahead of the pack? How can I beat the other guy before he beats me? Me. Me. Me.

My mom says it shouldn't be just me, me, me. It should also be thee, thee, thee. We should have the goal of serving others too. Not instead of serving ourselves. In addition to serving ourselves.

You gotta learn how to take good care of yourself. And when you learn how to take good care of yourself, then you can be at the top of your game. You can become the very best possible version of you. And then you can train yourself to be the very best kind of ... magnanimous.

It's funny, isn't it? When you improve yourself, you can start to transform. You can become the kind of person who is fully capable of taking really good care of the people around you. Better than you ever thought you could. And then – before you know it – everything around you gets better. And better and better and better. Ad infinitum.

You might even inspire other people to become the very best versions of themselves too. And what could ever be more magnanimous than that?

Personal Hygiene

Good! I'm glad you're here! The time has come! The hour has officially arrived!

At this particular juncture in time, we need to have a long-overdue conversation.

We need to address an uncomfortable topic. And you may not believe it, but this topic is as uncomfortable for me as it is for you.

Personal hygiene.

Yes, my friends, personal hygiene. Some of the kids in my school – even in my class – need to work on their personal hygiene. Failing to take care of your personal hygiene on a regular, daily schedule is one of the most *impersonal* things you can do. Because when you skip that shower ... and walk into the room smelling like a skunk in a thunderstorm ... you're not just disrespecting yourself, you're demonstrating a fundamental lack of consideration for your family, friends, and classmates.

See? Because it's not just about you.

It's like that new kid that sits next to me in math. He took his shoes off one day and I almost passed out. Wow! His bunions smelled like onions!

You don't want to treat your friends and neighbors like that, right? You don't want people around you experiencing anything that toxic, do you?

Of course not. So take a shower. Brush your teeth. Roll that deodorant. Roll it on thick. You want to smell good when you step out into the world.

The world will thank you for it. The world will welcome you with open arms. And open nostrils.

Intelligent Life

I saw that new science fiction movie with my friends last night. You know, the one everyone's been talking about ... with the flying pumpkins and the evil leprechauns from outer space. Well, not exactly leprechauns, but they look like leprechauns.

We went for ice cream after the movie. And we were talking about it for a long time. About how much of it was believable, and how much was completely unrealistic.

And this one kid – my friend's brother, who I had never even met before – said something that was totally out there. At first I thought he was joking. I was waiting for the punch line. But when I saw he was serious ... I felt like I had been punched!

This kid was serious ... and he said with a straight face –

"I think these films are important and socially relevant because they raise awareness of the everyday struggles experienced by leprechauns – not just in our country, but all over the world."

Wow. I mean, wow. Every jaw dropped. Every face went blank. Nobody knew what to say. Finally, my friend Sam broke the silence and said – *"All righty, then. I think it's time for us to get back to Planet Earth."*

I guess these movies are supposed to make people think ... and talk ... and question whether there may be intelligent life out there on other planets. But after what I heard last night ... it makes me wonder if there's intelligent life on this planet!

Not counting leprechauns, of course. But what do you think?

Mike Kimmel

It Is What It Is

It is what it is. Have you heard that? People say it all the time and I'm not even sure they know what they're saying. Not sure people understand the meaning. But if they do understand, then what they're really trying to say is ... *don't read too much into all the things you see going on around you.*

Because it is what it is.

Okay. If it is what it is, then it stands to reason the opposite is also true. It ain't what it ain't.

If it is what it is, then it ain't what it ain't.

That's an equally valid philosophy. It's equally important to remind ourselves that the things which may upset us, which may give us stress or make us nervous ... may not be all we imagine them to be.

Got a problem in life? Congratulations. Me too. Surprise, surprise, right? We've all got 'em. Those problems of yours may not be quite as horrific, quite as earth-shattering as you're building them up to be.

They may not be the big, bad bogeymen we've been picturing in our mind's eye. But ... if we imagine them to be overwhelming for us ... then that's our fault. That's on us. No problem is overwhelming unless we allow it to be. Don't be overwhelmed. Instead, just be whelmed.

Because it is what it is ... always has been. And it ain't what it ain't. Never will be.

The Me I'm Meant To Be

If I couldn't be me, then who would I be? Would I be thee? Or just a different version of me. Another kind of me.

Who would I be if my mother fell in love with a different man instead of my dad? Maybe her second choice. Would that make me a different kind of me? Maybe the second-best one of me? Or maybe my dad *was* her second choice. The one she settled for.

And if my mom hadn't settled, reduced herself, relegated herself to her own version of second- best, would I be a better, new and improved edition of me? Could I be all that I really could be? Everything I was ever supposed to be. What I was truly meant to be.

But maybe it doesn't matter who my mom fell in love with – or didn't. Same for my dad. Doesn't matter if my mom was his first choice or second choice. Or eleventh choice. What's most important are the choices *that I make.*

Because, in the end, who would *I want to be* if I couldn't be me? Maybe it's all up to me.

Maybe there's still time – if I *decide* there's time – for me to be the real me. The unique me. The true me. I decide. I decide. That's what determines who I am and who I will be.

Because in the end ... it's not up to he or she or thee. In the end, it's always up to me.

Can I Be Honest With You?

Can I be honest with you? Did you ever notice that when someone asks you that question … I mean, when they start a conversation with – *"Can I Be Honest With You?"* – what they're about to say is never good news?!

They're never gonna tell you how good looking you are, how madly in love with you they are, or how they want to buy you a pony. Or even a cupcake.

Instead, they want to tell you about all the mistakes you made. All the ways you let them down. And how deeply disappointed they are in you.

Well, they can't be *disappointed*. You know why? They were never *appointed*. I never appointed them. Nobody put these people in charge of our lives. My little sister says it best – *"You're not the boss of me!"* I agree with her!

So do me a favor, please. Don't be so honest with me! As a matter of fact, let me be honest with you. I want you to lie to me. Yes, lie to me. Build me up a little. Help me develop my self-esteem. Tell me how wonderful I am. Convince me I'm better than I am when I'm really not.

And if you really, truly feel the need to meddle in my life – crack open your piggy bank and buy me a pony. Or at least a little cupcake.

That would be very helpful. Honest, it would. Honest.

Sometimes ... It Just Isn't Right ...

We always want to try our best. You always want to make a situation turn out well if you can. But sometimes you can't force it. Sometimes you have to step away. Sometimes you have to get yourself out of a bad situation.

My father's really good at that. We went to this little pizza restaurant across town. Nothing fancy. Regular little place. We had never been there before. We had to wait a little while for a table. That's no biggie. We can wait.

But the workers weren't acting so friendly. And my dad didn't like their attitude. He decided we should go, and that's exactly what we did. My mom was embarrassed to walk out like that ... with everybody turning around and watching us leave.

Dad said he doesn't care what people think. Anybody who doesn't act nice is not gonna win his business. Plenty of other restaurants out there to choose from, right? Dad says he'd rather eat a cold, smelly hamburger in a good environment than filet mignon in a place where he's not welcome or appreciated.

I don't know about the cold, smelly hamburger part, but I think my dad's right on this one, and I give him credit for sticking to his principles.

A lot of people don't, you know? Sometimes you have to walk away. Because sometimes a situation is never gonna be right. And we can't make it right. So we shouldn't try and pretend it's right. Right?

The Mosquito Whisperer

D id I tell you I talk to mosquitoes? Yeah, that's right, I talk to mosquitoes. We were having a family cookout. A great time, but there were mosquitoes everywhere.

Everybody was getting bit, slapping their arms, slapping their legs. Looking for repellant, spraying themselves with stuff.

They all started looking at me ... asking why I'm not scratching.

I said because mosquitoes don't bite me. They break their beaks. They break their little pointers on me. And I talk to the mosquitoes, to all the assembled legions of mosquitoes. I say – *"Listen, you're just not gonna be able to do your little mosquito work here. You're gonna have to find someplace else to go ... and someone else to bite. If you bite me, you're gonna get bit back. I'll bite your little mosquito heads off."*

"Better go somewhere else. You're not wanted here, so hit the road, skeeters. All of you!

I'm not scared of you or what you can do to me. I wish you were bigger. Then you'd be more of a challenge. I wouldn't be afraid if you were the size of giant pterodactyls."

We gotta face our fears, not run from them. And not just with mosquitos at family cookouts, either. Talk to what's bothering you, and you can chase it away. That's why I don't use mosquito repellant. Don't need it. No, no, no, no no!

Mosquitoes need to spray something on them ... to protect their little fragile mosquito selves from me.

Get it? Got it? Good. Here endeth the lesson.

Unrealistic

I just met with my guidance counselor. Going over college admissions and stuff. You know what she told me? She said I was being unrealistic.

Unrealistic.

As I get older, more and more, I'm starting to feel … that it's important not to be so realistic in life. Because, from everything we've learned in school, nothing great was ever accomplished by a realist.

Personally, I think it's very unrealistic to step into a dark room, push a little piece of plastic from the down position to the up position … and all the lights come on. Like magic. To me, that's a very unrealistic idea.

When you think about it, unrealistic people are the ones we should model ourselves after. Unrealistic people are the citizens among us who really do the most extraordinary things in life.

So when people say it's unrealistic to become an actor, or play professional sports, or graduate at the top of your class, or get into the college of your choice … I love it!

That inspires me! That's gets me going. That's what makes me look for the next challenge. Because I don't want to just settle for normal or average. Normal is nice. But I'm making "*unrealistic*" my *goal* from now on.

Unrealistic is the new goal. Extraordinary is the new normal. And if you don't like it … then you're just not being realistic.

The Five-Minute Rule

I have to start with a bad word. Procrastination. We're all guilty of it. We put off doing those things we most need to do. We've become a procrastination nation. It's an abomination.

But I've got a solution to all that pollution.

A technique that's truly unique. To help you reach your peak. Whatever goal you may seek. But it's not for the meek.

I call it *The Five-Minute Rule*. Don't worry, it doesn't rhyme with anything.

Whatever you need to do, whatever you've been putting off ... do it for five minutes.

Don't try to do the whole job all at once. Five minutes of disciplined effort is enough.

I promise.

Five minutes studying. Five minutes cleaning your room. Five minutes exercising. Five minutes figuring out how to spend that next five minutes.

Because five minutes gets you into action. Five minutes of activity creates momentum. Momentum helps you take that next five-minute step. Before you know it, you're halfway done with that task you've been putting off. That way, it's not overwhelming. Don't be overwhelmed. Instead, just be whelmed.

Try it for five minutes. You can do anything for five minutes. Even change your way of attacking all those tasks you used to save for later.

Then you can stop and congratulate yourself. And that's a very nice way to spend five minutes.

Another Suggestion to Set You Apart

There's an unfortunate stereotype about young actors. Industry professionals believe young people know all about the current crop of actors, films, and television shows – but very little about those from years ago. This is truly a shame because show business has such a rich and fascinating history.

If you will take the time to research one old film, TV program, or actor from the past, I think you'll be amazed at how thoroughly you enjoy the experience. In fact, I suggest young people make this a regular practice. Make it part of your actor training. Try doing this every week and watch what happens. I bet you'll discover a whole new group of favorite actors who lit up the screen before your parents were even born. You'll discover movies and TV shows from years past that have many similarities to today's favorites. This is to be expected, because filmmakers often pay tribute to films that influenced and inspired them early in their careers.

Review the lists of actors, films, and television shows from years past on the following pages. You can write notes next to their names and keep a record of the stars and projects you like best. These are just starting points for you. There are far too many old-time greats to include them all, but this will give you a solid beginning. They are some of my all-time favorites.

Look up a few of them. Give them a fair chance. They may become some of your all-time favorites too.

"Life laughs at you when you are unhappy;
Life smiles at you when you are happy;
But life salutes you when you make others happy."

– Charlie Chaplin

Actors You Will Love

Bud Abbott and Lou Costello
Fred Astaire and Ginger Rogers
Lauren Bacall
Theda Bara
Lionel Barrymore
Ingrid Bergman
Humphrey Bogart
Clara Bow
Marlon Brando
Louise Brooks
Yul Brynner
James Cagney
Lon Chaney
Charlie Chaplin
Claudette Colbert
Gary Cooper
Joan Crawford
Tony Curtis
Dorothy Dandridge
Bette Davis
Doris Day
James Dean
Marlene Dietrich
Kirk Douglas
Douglas Fairbanks
W.C. Fields
Errol Flynn
Henry Fonda
Clark Gable
Greta Garbo
Dorothy and Lillian Gish
Jackie Gleason
Cary Grant

Paulette Goddard
Sidney Greenstreet
Jean Harlow
Rita Hayworth
Judy Holliday
Rock Hudson
James Earl Jones
Jennifer Jones
Audrey Hepburn
Katharine Hepburn
Charlton Heston
Boris Karloff
Buster Keaton
Grace Kelly
Veronica Lake
Hedy Lamarr
Burt Lancaster
Stan Laurel and Oliver Hardy
Harold Lloyd
Gina Lollobrigida
Carole Lombard
Sophia Loren
Peter Lorre
Myrna Loy
The Marx Brothers
Steve McQueen
Burgess Meredith
Marilyn Monroe
Paul Newman
Mabel Normand
Laurence Olivier
Gregory Peck
Mary Pickford

Zasu Pitts
Sidney Poitier
William Powell
Richard Pryor
Anthony Quinn
Donna Reed
Burt Reynolds
Debbie Reynolds
Edward G. Robinson
Mickey Rooney
Eva Marie Saint
George C. Scott
Peter Sellers
Sissy Spacek
Barbara Stanwyck
James Stewart
Gloria Swanson
Jessica Tandy
Elizabeth Taylor
Shirley Temple
Spencer Tracy
Jon Voight
Christopher Walken
John Wayne
Raquel Welch
Orson Welles
Mae West
Gene Wilder
Natalie Wood
Joanne Woodward

Must-See Movies

A Star is Born
American Graffiti
Anna Christie
The Blond Venus
Bus Stop
Casablanca
Citizen Kane
The Conversation
Cool Hand Luke
The Devil Doll
Freaks
Giant
The Freshman
The Goat
Gold Diggers of 1933
The Godfather
The Godfather Part II
The Gold Rush
Gone With The Wind
The Grapes of Wrath
Houdini
I Remember Mama
It Happened One Night
It's a Wonderful Life
The Kid
King Kong
Lifeboat
Limelight
Little Caesar
The Maltese Falcon
The Man Who Knew Too Much
The Man Who Would Be King
Marty

Mighty Joe Young
The Miracle Worker
The Misfits
Modern Times
The Most Dangerous Game
My Little Chickadee
North By Northwest
On the Waterfront
The Ox-Bow Incident
The Philadelphia Story
Portrait of Jennie
The Prince and the Showgirl
The Prizefighter and the Lady
The Public Enemy
Queen Christina
Requiem for a Heavyweight
Rocky
Rope
Scarlet Street
Sergeant York
Some Like it Hot
Speedy
Story of G.I. Joe
Sullivan's Travels
Sunset Boulevard
Trapeze
The Unholy Three
The Unknown
West Side Story
Westward the Women
Wild Bill: Hollywood Maverick
Wings
Yankee Doodle Dandy

Mike Kimmel

Terrific Vintage TV Shows

The Abbott and Costello Show
The Addams Family
The Adventures of Superman
Alfred Hitchcock Presents
All in the Family
The Andy Griffith Show
Batman
The Benny Hill Show
The Beverly Hillbillies
Bewitched
Big Valley
The Bionic Woman
Bonanza
Buffy The Vampire Slayer
The Carol Burnett Show
Car 54, Where Are You?
Columbo
The Courtship of Eddie's Father
The Dean Martin Celebrity Roast
Death Valley Days
The Dick Van Dyke Show
Dragnet
The DuPont Show of the Month
The Ed Sullivan Show
Family Affair
Father Knows Best
The Fugitive
The George Burns and Gracie Allen Show
Get Smart
Good Times
Green Acres
Gunsmoke
Happy Days

Herman's Head
Hill Street Blues
The Honeymooners
I Dream of Jeannie
I Love Lucy
I Married Joan
Ironside
It's About Time
The Jeffersons
Kolchak: The Night Stalker
Kraft Television Theatre
Lassie
Leave it to Beaver
The Lone Ranger
Lost in Space
Love, American Style
Magnum, P.I.
Make Room for Daddy
The Many Loves of Dobie Gillis
The Mary Tyler Moore Show
M*A*S*H
McHale's Navy
The Millionaire
The Milton Berle Show
The Mod Squad
The Monkees
Monty Python's Flying Circus
Mork and Mindy
Mr. Ed
The Munsters
My Favorite Martian
My Mother The Car
My Three Sons

Mystery Science Theater 3000
NYPD Blue
The Odd Couple
Our Miss Brooks
The Outer Limits
Perry Mason
Petticoat Junction
The Phil Silvers Show
Playhouse 90
Rhoda
The Rockford Files
Room 222
Rowan and Martin's Laugh-In
Sanford and Son
Seinfeld
77 Sunset Strip
The Six-Million Dollar Man
Star Trek
The Streets of San Francisco
Taxi
Three's Company
The Twilight Zone
The United States Steel Hour
Welcome Back, Kotter
The Wild, Wild West
WKRP in Cincinnati
The X-Files
Your Show of Shows
Zorro

About Jean Carol

Jean Carol is an Emmy Award Winner for *PM Magazine,* Emmy Nominee for *Guiding Light* (Best Supporting Actress), and recipient of a cast SAG Award for the Academy Award Winning Best Picture *Argo,* directed by Ben Affleck.

Jean started acting at age three on the New York stage in *Hansel and Gretel.* She was the youngest member of the Junior Theater Repertory Company at Carnegie Hall and performed there for seven seasons. Moving to Florida, she was crowned Miami's Junior Miss, Miss Teenage Miami, and Miss Miami. She earned her B.A. and M.S. degrees in theater and broadcasting at Florida State University, and began producing and hosting at NBC and CBS affiliates in Orlando and San Diego. At this time, she was selected as one of *GLAMOUR* magazine's Outstanding Young Working Women, and inducted into their Hall of Fame.

During her seven year, 795 episode run as Nadine Cooper on *Guiding Light,* Jean won a fan favorite *Soap Opera Digest* Award for Outstanding Newcomer, and 4 Nominations for Best Comic Performance, Best Supporting Actress, Best Scene Stealer, and was named one of Daytime Television's All Time Favorite Funny Ladies. Jean starred as Catherine Devon in 146 episodes of the drama series *Ocean Avenue.* Other screen credits include *The Mentalist, Monk, Working Class, Six Feet Under, Arli$$, Vanilla Sky, Payback,* and a co-starring role alongside Jane Seymour in the CBS Movie of the Week, *A Memory In My Heart.*

Jean filmed 1500-plus episodes over six years as Host and Producer on *PM Magazine,* interviewing celebrities from Cathy Rigby to Clint Eastwood. She won an Emmy, received four more Emmy Nominations for writing, producing and performing, and a National Best Feature Story Award. She hosted HSN's *Great Escapes* travel series, *ESPN's Ski Scene: Ski Austria,* and *Healthy Lifestyles* with Olympic gold medalist Bruce (aka Caitlyn) Jenner for three years.

Jean lives in L.A. with her husband, actor Gerry Rand, and their three spoiled dogs. The couple is dedicated to animal rescue.

113

About Mike Kimmel

Mike Kimmel is a film, television, stage, and commercial actor and acting coach. He is a twenty-plus year member of SAG-AFTRA with extensive experience in both the New York and Los Angeles markets. He has worked with directors Francis Ford Coppola, Robert Townsend, Craig Shapiro, and Christopher Cain among many others. TV credits include *Game of Silence, Zoo, Treme, In Plain Sight, Cold Case, Breakout Kings, Memphis Beat,* and *Buffy The Vampire Slayer.* He was a regular sketch comedy player on *The Tonight Show,* performing live on stage and in pre-taped segments with Jay Leno for eleven years.

Mike has appeared in dozens of theatrical plays on both coasts, including Radio City Music Hall, Equity Library Theater, Stella Adler Theater, Double Image Theater, and Theater at the Improv. He trained with Michael Shurtleff, William Hickey, Ralph Marrero, Gloria Maddox, Harold Sylvester, Wendy Davis, Amy Hunter, Bob Collier, and Stuart Robinson. He has a B.A. from Brandeis University and an M.A. from California State University.

As an educator, he has taught at Upper Iowa University, University of New Orleans, University of Phoenix, Nunez Community College, Delgado Community College, and in the Los Angeles, Beverly Hills, and Burbank, California public school districts. He is a two-time past president of New Orleans Toastmasters, the public speaking organization, and often serves as an international speech contest judge. Mike has written and collaborated on numerous scripts for stage and screen. *In Lincoln's Footsteps,* his full-length historical drama on Presidents Lincoln and Garfield, was a 2013 semi-finalist in the National Playwrights Conference at the Eugene O'Neill Theater Center. He is the 2014 recipient of the Excellence in Teaching Award from Upper Iowa University.

Mike is a voting member of the Academy of Television Arts and Sciences and the author of *Scenes for Teens* and *Acting Scenes for Kids and Tweens.*

"To hold our tongues when everyone is gossiping,
to smile without hostility at people and institutions,
to compensate for the shortage of love in the world
with more love in small, private matters;
to be more faithful in our work, to show greater patience,
to forgo the cheap revenge obtainable from mockery
and criticism: all these are things we can do."

– Hermann Hesse

CPSIA information can be obtained
at www.ICGtesting.com
Printed in the USA
LVHW05s1453051018
592550LV00009B/500/P

9 780998 151311